JOHN CLARE

FLOWER POEMS

For my parents

Istvan and Pauline Kövesi

JOHN CLARE

FLOWER POEMS

Edited by Simon Kövesi
Oxford Brookes University

M&C Services, Bangkok
2001

John Clare (1793-1864)
Flower Poems

Edited with an Introduction and Glossary by Simon Kövesi

First Edition, 2001

Published by
M&C Services
806, 7th floor
Riverhouse Condominium
Ladya Road, Kheang Klongsan
Bangkok, Thailand

Typeset by Simon Kövesi

Printed by Bell and Bain Ltd, Glasgow

Cover photography copyright © Peter Moyse A.R.P.S. 2001

For distribution: http://human.ntu.ac.uk/clare/love.html
Email: kovesi@hotmail.com

ISBN 974 87960 9 4

COPYRIGHT
With the exception of the cover images, no copyright whatsoever is claimed or maintained to any part of this publication, by neither the editor nor the publisher.

CONTENTS

Acknowledgements	viii
Introduction	ix
Notes to Introduction	xxiii
The Primrose, A Sonnet	1
To an Insignificant Flower Obscurely Blooming in a Lonely Wild	2
Violet – Thou Art a Holy Blossom	4
To the Violet	5
To a Cowslip Early	6
Sonnet: To a Red Clover Blossom	7
Ballad ('A weedling wild on lonely lea')	8
The humble flower that buds upon the plain	9
Song ('Swamps of wild rush beds and slough's squashy traces')	10
Thrice Welcome Sweet Summer in Softness Returning	11
O Native Scenes, Nought to My Heart Clings Nearer	12
A Wild Nosegay	13
There's the Daisy, the Woodbine	14
On Some Friends Leaving a Favourite Spot	15
Faery Elves, those Minute Things	19
A Walk ('The thorn tree just began to bud')	20
Mild Health I Seek Thee, Whither Art Thou Found?	21
The Daisy Wan, the Primrose Pale	22
Childhood	23
The Anniversary, To a Flower of the Desert	37
The Holiday Walk	39

Sport in the Meadows	48
The Eternity of Nature	50
The Evergreen Rose	53
The Primrose Bank	54
On Seeing Some Moss in Flower Early in Spring	57
Ballad: ('The spring returns, the pewet screams')	59
Summer Ballad	61
Idle Hour	65
A Spring Morning	66
Another Spring: The Crab Tree	67
Scraps of Summer	68
The Poesy of Flowers	69
A Woodland Seat	70
The Evening Primrose	72
Sonnet: Forest Flowers	73
The Fear of Flowers	74
First Sight of Spring	75
Pleasant Spots	76
The Clump of Fern	77
The Yarrow	78
The Ragwort	79
The Bramble	80
Heavy Dew	81
The Hedge Woodbine	82
The Water Lilies on the Meadow Stream	83
Spring ('The sweet spring now is coming')	84
Valentine ('A dewdrop on a rose leaf')	86
To E. L. E. on May Morning	87
The Nosegay of Wild Flowers	91
Field Thoughts	94
Open Winter	95
The Little Paths are Printed Every One	96
When Milking Comes then Home the Maiden Wends	97

The Dreary Fen a Waste of Water Goes	98
A Walk ('Being refreshed with thoughts of wandering moods')	99
The Daisy	102
Editorial Note	103
Glossary and Notes	106
Index	112

ACKNOWLEDGEMENTS

I would like to thank the staff of the National Library of Thailand, the Nottingham Trent University Library at Clifton, the Peterborough Museum and Art Gallery, the Northampton Central Library, the University of Dundee Library, the University of Glasgow Library and the British Library.

I would like to thank the Peterborough Museum and Art Gallery and the Northampton Central Library for permission to transcribe from their manuscript collections. I am also grateful to Microform Academic Publishers, Wakefield, for allowing me to transcribe from its microfilm edition of the Clare manuscripts.

Michael Gorman of M&C Services has been resolutely encouraging over the course of an interesting two years since the publication of *Love Poems* in July 1999. For her patient administrative assistance I would like to thank Chitratree Chararinchai of M&C Services in Bangkok. The research for this selection was funded by M&C Services, with additional funds allocated by the Department of English at the University of Dundee, for which I am very grateful. For the cover images I am indebted to the Honorary Secretary of the John Clare Society, Mr Peter Moyse, A.R.P.S..

I have relied upon many people for advice and help in working towards this edition, and in dealing with reactions to the last one, including Ben Ackland, Kasia Boddy, Philip Clarkstone, Bob Cummings, John Goodridge, Nick Groom, Tracey Herd, Peter Kitson, Sonya Kövesi, Alex, Sam and Alfie Macdonald, Alison Ramsden, Nick Roe, Jane Stabler, Judith Summerfield and Simon Wood. Special thanks go to Nessa Curran who kindly proofed part of the text for me and to Brendan Doherty and Iain Sim for their vital technical assistance.

While I believe John Clare's work is resolutely his own, I would like to dedicate this edition of it to my parents, Istvan and Pauline Kövesi, with all my love.

Simon Kövesi
Govan, Glasgow
August 2001

INTRODUCTION

But now she surpasses all the women
of Lydia, like the moon,
rose-fingered, after the sun has set,

shining brighter than all the stars; its light
stretches out over the salt-
filled sea and the fields brimming with flowers.

the beautiful dew falls and the roses
and the delicate chervil
and many-flowered honey-clover blossom.[1]

In Sappho's lines above, the colour of the rose is used to describe the sky. The image is enriched by both the tactile 'fingers' of the personified dawn, and the implicit fragrance and delicacy of the bloom. She then paints a scene with a vividness that, before artificial dyes and fragrances were commonplace, could only have been available to her through the chervil and the honey-clover blossom.[2] And therein lies the attraction of the flower for the poet: the combination of a rare colour, with a delicate scent, together with an easily-recognisable visualisation for the reading audience. For millennia this is a combination which has proven itself irresistible to any poet concerned with intimacy, sensuality, nature or love. The intricate structural patterns and forms of flowers seem somehow to reflect and inform the formal qualities of verse. As Emily Dickinson humbly puts it, flowers

Have a system of aesthetics –
Far superior to mine.[3]

Flowers also provide a wealth of associative metaphors, and so flower-lore is as rich and various as the history of literature. Indeed, literary history is so closely connected with flora that I could have started this introduction with any poet, of any tradition, and in any language. The very word 'anthology' stems from the Greek for a gathering or collection of flowers. From the earliest years of British poetry publishing, anthologies of verse have had titles such as *England's Parnassus: or The Choysest Flowers of our Moderne Poets* (1600).[4] (In publishing terms, 'the flowers' came to mean 'the best bits', not just of selections of verse, but also of selections of prose, letters and scientific works.) Equally, many botanical and horticultural guides, right up to Richard Mabey's magnificent *Flora Britannica* of 1996,[5] contain explanatory quotations from the poets. In publishing terms then, flowers and poetry have often gone hand in hand. And for poets such as Robert Bloomfield, Leigh Hunt and John Imlah,[6] contemporaries of John Clare, flowers are an overarching theme, a unifying topic. For poets flowers can provide a mode of public presentation. Flowers have consistently been as central to the role and performance of the poet, and to his or her presentation to the public, as any other feature of the natural world.

For the Romantic-period poet, the flower offered a number of differing attractions. Specifically for John Keats[7] and fellow Cockney-school members like Leigh Hunt, flowers form a gaudy, sensual backdrop. In their verse, flowers are invested with a ritualised eroticism which indirectly echoes the lines of Sappho above, but more directly alludes to other, predominantly male, classical authors. Indeed, the use of flowers to convey a pagan orgy of colour was one of many unpalatable aspects for the Cockney poets' contemporary reviewers, and flowery-bowery poems such as Keats's 'I stood tip-toe upon a little hill' epitomized the ravings of what was dismissed as the 'suburban school' of poetry:[8]

> I gazed awhile, and felt as light, and free
> As though the fanning wings of Mercury
> Had played upon my heels: I was light-hearted,
> And many pleasures to my vision started;

INTRODUCTION

> So I straightway began to pluck a posey
> Of luxuries bright, milky, soft and rosy
>
> A bush of May flowers with the bees about them;
> Ah, sure no tasteful nook would be without them;
> And let a lush laburnum oversweep them,
> And let long grass grow round the roots to keep them
> Moist, cool and green; and shade the violets,
> That they might bind the moss in leafy nets.[9]

Here the flowers provide a stimulating springboard for the flight of the poet's fancy. His entranced gaze upon the fecund natural scene begins his classical allusiveness, and thence his sensual vision alights upon the flowers of spring. It is no coincidence that Keats spells 'posy' with an 'e'; 'posey' is so close to 'poesy' (the archaic version of 'poetry' that Keats employs frequently) orthographically and aurally that it almost requires a double-take of the reader – both meanings of both words are immediately present. The poem is rendered as organically and freely-born as a flower.

Keats was first published by John Clare's publishing firm Taylor and Hessey. The publisher had a fair bit of trouble in managing the idiosyncrasies of both poets. In Keats's case, John Taylor and James Hessey were simply not prepared for the vicious reactionary reviewers, who mostly detested the poet's florid paganism, and what they saw as his pretensions to an aroused and poorly-informed classicism; for Clare, the publisher had to mediate between a predominantly middle-class, London-based audience and a poet whose knowledge of flowers, enjoyment of botany and indulgence in his Northamptonshire dialect were unprecedented. As Margaret Grainger notes, when it comes to the natural world 'Clare makes no distinctions between what is fit subject for poetry and what is not';[10] in other words, Clare did not exclude anything if it was worthy of his attention, and he was to some extent deliberately heedless of the fashionable literary tastes of his time. In verse, he did his own thing; in the natural world of his village of Helpston and its environs, every element was worthy of his attentive, informed eye.

It is worth considering for a moment just how much Clare knew about his local flora and how dependent upon his local soil his poetic life was. The sister-in-law of Leigh Hunt, Elizabeth Kent[11] (also published by Taylor and Hessey), wrote in her *Flora Domestica* of 1823 that no poet had 'better understood the language of flowers' than Clare.[12] So well did Clare know the flora of Britain that he was able to see the faults and omissions in the urban Kent's encyclopaedic literary anthology.[13] But he was also delighted to be one of the most lengthily-quoted poets in the book, if slightly embarrassed. To James Hessey, Clare wrote:

> I am pleased with the mention the author has made of me, and not only pleased, but proud of it. I will make a few remarks while I am hot, for I shall soon be cold perhaps. How pretty is the allusion to poor Keats's grave! Hazlitt says, the early writers described flowers the best; perhaps they do; and, I think, they are mentioned too sparingly, and the living ones almost (will vanity let me own it) too much. Milton is a capital painter of them, and Cowley, when he does mention them, does it finely, often in spite of his conceits. Our Shakspeare—no, the world will not let him be ours any longer—well, the world's Shakspeare sounds better—he has some bewitching pictures of them, sweeter even (if it is possible) than Nature herself: and my favourite Thomson shall not yield to any one, either ancient or modern, in my opinion—only mine perhaps.[14]

He goes on to criticise a mistake in Kent's entry for the cowslip (one of Clare's favourite flowers, which he called a 'cowslap'). This letter reveals a poet who knows his contemporaries' work very well indeed, but also a poet who has a refined knowledge of poetic tradition. It is also clear that Clare is flattered by his appearance alongside poets he reveres. Kent's book must have considerably increased Clare's confidence in his art at a crucial, formative time in his writing career. Kent was the first in a long line of anthologisers to recognise just how rich and accurate was Clare's understanding of floral England. She was also the first critic to discuss him alongside Geoffrey Chaucer, William Wordsworth and Percy Bysshe Shelley. Of her friend Shelley, she romanticises:

INTRODUCTION

...it was his delight to ramble out into the fields and woods, where he would take his book, or sometimes his pen, and having employed some hours in study, and in speculations on his favourite theme – the advancement of human happiness, would return home with his hat wreathed with briony, or wild convolvulus; his hand filled with bunches of wild-flowers plucked from the hedges as he passed, and his eyes, indeed every feature, beaming with the benevolence of his heart (p. xix).

That Clare would have been aware of Shelley's work this early in his career is a commonly-ignored fact in Clare studies.[15] But it is towards the end of her Introduction to *Flora Domestica*, where she reaches a concluding rapture over her subject, that Kent eventually turns to Clare:

And flowers do speak a language, a clear and intelligible language: ask Mr. Wordsworth, for to him they have spoken, until they excited "thoughts that lie too deep for tears;" ask Chaucer, for he held companionship with them in the meadows; ask any of the poets, ancient or modern. Observe them, reader, love them, linger over them; and ask your own heart if they do not speak affection, benevolence, and piety. None have better understood the language of flowers than the simple-minded peasant-poet, Clare, whose volumes are like a beautiful country, diversified with woods, meadows, heaths, and flower-gardens... (pp. xxi-xxii).

If such vaulted praise is heartening, Kent's presentation of the poet as 'simple-minded' is highly problematic for today's readership and suggests the intractable stratification of the class divide that gulfed between the urban middle-class Kent and the rural labouring-class Clare. But his letter to James Hessey (above) and his subsequent display of avian expertise in his assisting of Kent with her *History of Birds*[16] are testament to the fact that Clare was far from being simple-minded.

Clare was himself a 'wild flower'[17] for the contemporary literary scene of his time; a self-taught, 'natural genius' who grew up in one of the wildest, parochial, villages in England and he was marketed as such by Taylor and Hessey. While he came to resent such limiting marketing in time, he was also keen to utilise the idiosyncrasies of his locality and its associated rural, often floriferous, customs. For his planned volume *The Midsummer Cushion* he introduced his poems as if they were themselves a rural, local offering of flowers, ritualistically but naturally produced from the soil of Northamptonshire. In his prose Introduction, Clare explains:

> It is a very old custom among villagers in summertime to stick a piece of greensward full of field flowers and place it as an ornament in their cottages, which ornaments are called 'Midsummer Cushions'. And these trifles are field flowers of humble pretensions of various hues. I thought the above cottage custom gave me an opportunity to reflect a title that was not inapplicable to the contents of the Volume – not that I wish the reader to imagine that by doing so I consider these poems in the light of flowers that can even ornament a cottage by their presence. Yet if the eye of beauty can feel even an hour's entertainment in their perusal I shall take it as the proudest of praise and if the lover of simple images and rural scenery finds anything to commend, my end and aim is gratified.[18]

The village custom he describes in his Introduction, continues to this day in a different form, every year on or near July 13, the poet's birthday. Now, the cushions of local flowers, prepared in green seed trays by the children of the John Clare School in Helpston, are laid to rest around the poet's gravestone. Satisfyingly then, the poet, his place and his flowers are bound together in a unique ritual by the local children. This annual commemoration is even more significant in that the theme of childhood and memories of its freedom are frequently provoked in Clare's work by flowers. Children make *use* of flowers; in their hands wild flowers become much more than simply sentimental or decorative ornaments. For Clare flowers help children imagine and enthuse, and aid them in their play, their colours and shapes suggesting to and provoking nascent and active imaginations. In 'Childhood' flowers are toys, along with anything else the children can pilfer:

> The stonecrop that on ruins comes
> And hangs like golden balls,
> How oft to reach its shining blooms
> We scaled the mossy walls;

INTRODUCTION

>And weeds – we gathered weeds as well
> Of all that bore a flower,
>And tied our little posies up
> Beneath the eldern bower.
>
>Our little gardens there we made
> Of blossoms all a-row,
>And though they had no roots at all
> We hoped to see them grow;
>And in the cart rut after showers
> Of sudden summer rain,
>We filled our tiny water pots
> And cherished them in vain.
>
>We pulled the moss from apple trees
> And gathered bits of straws,
>When weary twirling of our tops
> And shooting of our taws;
>We made birds' nests and thought that birds
> Would like them ready-made,
>And went full twenty times a day
> To see if eggs were laid.

In that same word 'posies' which Keats employs above in 'I stood tip-toe upon a little hill', we can see the vast difference between the two poets' interests and their contrasting utilisation of the natural world. Where Keats is classical and ever-tending upwards towards a sensual sublime, Clare is local, pragmatic and his vision seems to be level with the ground. Where the flowers in Keats's poetry are used, more often than not, for sexual or sensual metaphor, in Clare's the flowers are more often tangible things to be considered for their own sake. Both poets though have a heightened awareness of touch and an intimate delicacy which is all their own; both also have an essentially post-Wordsworthian ecstatic sense of joy in humanity's interaction with nature. But Clare deliberately moves away from the tradition of using flowers in verse as literary symbol or metaphorical backdrop. Of course he does use their sexual function and romantic connotations, especially in love poems, but rather like the children of his poem, he often interacts with them in a material and tactile fashion, in contrast to his contemporaries.

In the memory of an older man in Clare's poetry, flowers are able to hold on to the most significant and private moments of his past (see especially 'Flowers and Spring'[19]). For the older poet, the cyclical return of colourful blooms is as predictable and irrepressible as the return of permanent memories of the past. As Ronald Blythe recently put it, Clare writes of 'the past as though it were the present... [He is] a remembrancer'.[20] So flowers repeatedly provoke memories in Clare's verse, and often those memories are painfully remote, yet sharply conveyed. If Clare's relationship with flowers seems ambivalent because of the pain they can cause his memory, that relationship consistently remains impassioned and conveyed with an alert clarity. The final poem in this volume 'The Daisy' dates from 1860 and is one of Clare's last extant poems. It reveals that to the end of his life his vision of nature was as naturally floral as it had always been, even after nineteen years of confinement in the clipped, hedged and trimmed lawns of the Northampton Genral Lunatic Asylum.

Clare writes in his own language of flowers. He does not dwell sentimentally upon a folkloric, superstitious floral world used just for symbol and metaphor. Nor is he particularly interested in easily-cultivated, domesticated flowers. In many poems, his stance against the commonly-known flower of the comfortable home becomes political, as in these lines from 'The Holiday Walk':

> See there sit the swath summer lovers at play
> Neath the shade of those broad spreading maples all day,
>   Those brown tawny lasses with lips like a cherry
>   And fair full as dark as the autumn blackberry;
> The mole hillocks make them soft cushions for love
> And the hedges in harbours hang blooming above.
>   As blessed as the rich who on sofas reposes,
>   They toy neath the shades of wild woodbines and roses.

The natural world offers pleasures to the rural poor which make them 'blessed' like the rich. But a political distinction is made, and it is a slightly embittered one. Perhaps the point is that the rich could not understand such pleasures because they are not forced to seek them; nor perhaps would they feel it appropriate to make love outside. For Clare, that is their loss. This passage is as close as Clare comes to the sensual floridity of Keats and Hunt, the main difference lying in its – albeit soft-focussed – social realism and rural immediacy. 'The Holiday Walk' is allusive to literary tradition, but to a specifically rural one. The last lines of the poem read:

> I'll reach down a poet I love from the shelves
>   My Thomson or Cowper like flowers in their prime,
>   That sat not in closets to study and rhyme,
>   But roamed out of doors for their verses that yield
>   A freshness like that which we left in the field;
>   That sing both at once to the ear and the eye
>   And breathe of the air and the grass and the sky
>   A music so sweet while we're hid from the rain
>   That we even seem taking our rambles again.

Here Clare deftly conflates the reading of nature with the reading of the nature poetry of James Thomson, author of *The Seasons* (1730) – the book of poetry which Clare claims started him writing in the first place – and William Cowper, author of the meditative and predominantly rural poem *The Task* (1785). The poets are possessed by Clare in that 'my'; they are *his* now. Like him, he says, they were active in seeking their poetic inspiration 'in the field'. And still, decades after their deaths, these poets are 'like flowers in their prime'. For Clare, an avid reader of English poetry, their clarity and potential are undiminished by time. Clare's own desire to join these immortal ranks is not classicised: it is English, naturalised, rural and modest.

Where Clare wishes to emulate, he does not copy. He differs from any poet before him in his construction of a world of flowers in which the tiniest details of colour, sexuality, difference and form are acutely, sensitively and knowledgeably understood. Furthermore, unlike his poetic forbears Thomson and Cowper, Clare knew the groundbreaking scientific work of his near-contemporaries Carolus Linnaeus (the Swedish botanist about whose classification system Clare felt ambivalent[21]) and Erasmus Darwin (author of *The Botanic Garden*, 1789). In his research for *The Flora of Northamptonshire,* George Claridge Druce wrote in 1930 that:

In [Clare's] poems about a hundred and twenty different plants are referred to, and of these about forty-two are mentioned for the first time as Northamptonshire species. In reading his poems again for the purpose of compiling this notice, one has been frequently impressed with Clare's close and accurate information; if the Muse had not claimed him for her own, Natural Science would have gained a devotee.[22]

Druce goes on to list 135 varieties of flowers which he identifies in Clare's published works up to 1930. So Clare was a botanist and a naturalist – but he was also someone who knew the soil and its life intimately, and someone who had first-hand experience of microcosmic ecosystems, and humanity's relationship with and effect upon them. To some degree Clare is the Romantic poet of the microcosm, and of miniature ecosystems. This is not to say that his poetry is less relevant for twenty-first-century readers than the more epic eye of poets of nature, like William Wordsworth. There is perhaps a case to support the possibility that at times, Clare's poetic eye is more visually focused. In Clare's poetry, flowers are rarely grouped together in a group of 'ten thousand' as they are in Wordsworth's 'Daffodils'. A 'host of dancing daffodils'[23] is a blurry kingdom which establishes an impression of colour and movement rather than an intimate portrait of an individual flower. Wordsworth's portrait of the flowers is indeed meant to be an impression conveyed through recollection. The portrait of flowers in this particular poem might also lack immediacy and focus because the image of the daffodils was recollected not from William Wordsworth's own memory, but from an acquisitive reading of his sister Dorothy's much more detailed journal entry.[24] Interestingly, the detail of that journal entry reads rather like Clare's natural history accounts, as Margaret Grainger has noted.[25] Clare's natural vision is perhaps closer to Dorothy Wordsworth's than it is to her brother's. It might be then that Clare's natural vision is closer to the female nature writers of his day than it is to any of his male contemporaries; certainly he shows no gender prejudice in his reading, unlike that of his male contemporaries. Maybe his eye, when turned upon nature, lacks the gendered dimension of his contemporaries.

INTRODUCTION

Where William Wordsworth's eye is egotistically imperious, Clare's could be said to be democratic. Where John Keats feels the daisies growing over him on his deathbed, or senses them at his feet in the darkness of internalised transcendence,[26] it seems that Clare puts his eye as close as he can to the 'eye' of the flower. To quote Ronald Blythe again, Clare 'despised those who were blind to the flowers beneath their feet.'[27] Clare delights in the particularities of the under-appreciated, the ignored, the uncultivated and the wild. His poems recover unknown flowers from obscurity, and weeds from human prejudice, just as his tales of rural life foreground the marginal and the dispossessed in human society. He revels too in untouched and wild greenery, even when not in flower. Clare's natural vision is actually rare in *not* requiring flowers as nodes of interest and in this respect, his vision is indeed close to Dorothy Wordsworth's. She writes keenly of flowers but, like Clare, she seems equally set against excessive floridity:

> There, too, in many a sheltered chink
> The foxglove's broad leaves flourished fair,
> And silver birch whose purple twigs
> Bend to the softest breathing air.
>
> What need of flowers? The splendid moss
> Is gayer than an April mead –
> More rich its hues of varied green,
> Orange and gold, and glowing red.[28]

Although Clare read a great many female poets,[29] he makes no explicit reference to Dorothy Wordsworth's work as it remained largely unpublished in his lifetime. He did however read a great deal of her brother's work. The following stanza of Clare's from 'The Nosegay of wild flowers', though clearly derivative of Charlotte Smith's 'Nosegay of Wild Flowers',[30] bears a significant affinity to William Wordsworth's 'Lines Written a Few Miles above Tintern Abbey':

> 'Tis sweet to view as in a favoured book
>   Life's rude beginning page long turned o'er;

'Tis nature's common feeling back to look
  On things that pleased us when they are no more,
Pausing on childish scenes a wished repeat,
  Seeming more sweet to value when we're men
As one awakened from a vision sweet
  Wisheth to sleep and dream it o'er again.

In Clare's sense of the elevated 'value' in beholding the natural world as an adult rather than as a child, we might hear Wordsworth's '[a]bundant recompense' for the older, wiser poet who, compared to the period of his 'thoughtless youth', is now able to hear the 'still, sad music of humanity' with a richer comprehension.[31] However, Clare's poem differs from William Wordsworth's in its intimate portrayal of tiny scenes, and in images such as the '[c]rimp-frilled daisy, bright bronze buttercup'; Wordsworth rarely indulges his grandly ambitious psychological vista with such minutiae. Where Wordsworth counts the five years[32] since his last visit to Tintern (lines 1–2), in 'The Eternity of Nature' Clare counts the number five he sees suddenly everywhere, in a cabalistic, frenzied delight in nature's 'strange' mystery:

With the odd number five strange nature's laws
Plays many freaks nor once mistakes the cause,
  And in the cowslap peeps this very day
  Five spots appear which time ne'er wears away,
Nor once mistakes the counting. Look within
Each peep and five nor more nor less is seen,
  And trailing bindweed with its pinky cup
  Five lines of paler hue goes streaking up;
And birds-a-merry keep the rule alive
And lay five eggs nor more nor less than five;
  And flowers how many own that mystic power
  With five leaves ever making up the flower;
The five-leaved grass trailing its golden cups
Of flowers – five leaves make all for which I stoop
  And briony in the hedge that now adorns
  The tree to which it clings and now the thorn's
Own five-star-pointed leaves of dingy white:
Count which I will, all make the number right.

In the defamiliarising mystery of pattern, Clare finds evidence of divinity, of a maker. In looking so closely at nature, in counting spots, lines, patterns and shapes on petals, leaves, and blades of grass, Clare breaks all the rules of eighteenth-century English nature poetry. He also breaks away from his contemporaries. His sight is not myopic, but as this poem suggests, it is more detailed than Wordsworth's in terms of the visual vividness and acuity of its rural scenes. And when Clare's mind is engaging with nature in such intimacy, it lacks the hierarchy that always exists in William Wordsworth's poetry, I think, between man and nature. Of course both poets could in part be expressing the internalised imagery of their varying geographical locations, which might in some ways have impacted upon their psychological development as children and so their poetical vision as adults (in *The Prelude* Wordsworth certainly thinks this is the case). Clare's Helpston is not situated on flat fen land and does have gentle hills and possible views, but he never witnessed any view so grand as the mountains of Wordsworth's Lake District (the furthest place north Clare visited was Nottingham). More readily to Clare comes a vision which has no top or bottom, no grand ego at the height, nor with God's (nor the poet's) glory spread out *beneath* him. It is worth noting that the 1798 'Lines' of Wordsworth's were composed 'a Few Miles *above* Tintern Abbey'. It is hard to imagine Clare coining such a title.

Where William Wordsworth and Keats look for symbols of themselves in nature, Clare's interest is in natural things in themselves, for their own sake first and foremost. Flowers and nature in Clare's work are expressed with a suddenness; they are conveyed with a vital rushing to be expressed and with immediacy. Of course there is plan and pattern in Clare's vision, reflecting the plethora of patterns he sees in nature. But he deliberately avoids any hierarchical schema and avoids, by and large, placing his own consciousness on centre stage. Where he puts himself in the frame, he does so with a faltering modesty and seeming reluctance that is quintessentially Clarean, not (William–) Wordsworthian, Keatsian, Shelleyan or Byronic.

Although the oft-quoted 'Wordsworthian shadow' from which Harold Bloom thought Clare never emerged is more sensibly seen as a 'Wordsworthian light', Clare develops his own coherent, individual vision which sets him apart from his contemporaries. His vision of nature is to some degree Romantic but it is also a vision which is so detailed, so botanically and socially knowledgeable and – especially by the 1830s and *The Midsummer Cushion* poems – so refined, honed and yet still so immediate – that really we must begin to see Clare not as a failed or marginal Romantic, nor even a 'counterromantic'[33] but as someone who successfully amalgamates traditions and influences from the nature poetry of Theocritus; the love poetry of Ovid; the sensual eye of Robert Herrick and John Suckling; the 'green' eye of Andrew Marvell; the detailed rural eye and social awareness of James Thomson, William Cowper and Robert Bloomfield; the ballads of Allan Ramsay, Robert Burns, James Hogg and Allan Cunningham; the sonnets of Charlotte Smith; the botanising of Erasmus Darwin; the romantic isolation of Johann Wolfgang von Goethe's Werther; the varying egocentricities of William Wordsworth and Byron; the Romance of Walter Scott, and the youthful, idealistic and political heat of Percy Bysshe Shelley and John Keats. All of these influences and many more can be unearthed in Clare. But what he creates from and sometimes against such a wealth of reading, in combination with his unprecedented understanding of nature, is as convincing a portrait of the natural world in verse as can be found anywhere in English literature.

INTRODUCTION

NOTES TO INTRODUCTION

¹ From fragment 33, in *Sappho: Poems and Fragments*, trans. Josephine Balmer (Newcastle: Bloodaxe Books, 1992), p. 47.
² Although, as Germaine Greer points out 'Sappho is supposed to have called herself Psappha, a word meaning, if after a millennium or three we can be sure of anything so fugitive as a word meaning, lapis lazuli' (*Slip-Shod Sybils: Recognition, Rejection and the Woman Poet*, London: Penguin, 1996, p. 103). *Lapis lazuli* is both the name of a valued mineral, and a bright blue pigment.
³ Emily Dickinson, 'Flowers – Well – if anybody', no. 137 (*The Complete Poems*, ed. Thomas H. Johnson, London: Faber & Faber, 1975), p. 64. This poem was probably written in 1859, five years before Clare died.
⁴ The full title is *Englands Parnassus: or The Choysest Flowers of our Moderne Poets, with their Poeticall comparisons*, ed. Robert Allott (London: N. Ling, C. Burke and T. Hayes, 1600). More recent examples might include *Flowers of British Poetry,Consisting of Fugitive and Classical Pieces of the Best Poets of Great Britain*, [anon.] (Newcastle on Tyne: J. Mitchell, ca. 1802); *Wild Flowers; or, a Selection of original poetry*, ed. John Lyth (London: Hamilton, Adams & Co., 1843); *Songs, Madrigals and Sonnets: A gathering of some of the most pleasant flowers of old English poetry*, ed. Joseph Cundall, (London, Longman & Co., 1849); *Flowers from Shakespeare's Garden; a Posy from the Plays*, ed. Walter Crane (London: Cassell, 1906).
⁵ Richard Mabey, *Flora Britannica* (London: Sinclair-Stevenson, 1996). Cf. *Flora Poetica, or poetry on flowers*, ed. Thomas Willcocks (London: Longman, Rees, Orme and Co., 1835) or *The Dictionary of Poetry and of Flowers*, Henry Gardiner Adams (London: Dean & Son, 1856).
⁶ Robert Bloomfield, *Wild Flowers; or Pastoral and Local Poetry* (London: Vernor, Hood, etc., 1806); Leigh Hunt, *Foliage; or Poems Original and Translated* (London: C. and J. Ollier, 1818); John Imlah, *May Flowers, Poems and Songs: Some in the Scottish Dialect*, (London, 1827); also see Maria Henrietta Montolieu, *The Enchanted Plants, and Festival of the Rose; with other poems* (London, 1812) *The Ladies' Hand-Book of the Language of Flowers*, ed. Lucy Hooper (London, 1844) for examples of the many botanic and poetic works by women.
⁷ Cf. Keats's 'O come, dearest Emma! The rose is full blown', 'To Leigh Hunt,

xxiii

Esq.', 'Hither, hither, love' and *Endymion.*
[8] See Bewell, Alan J., 'Keats's "Realm of Flora"', *Studies in Romanticism,*(1992) 31(1), pp. 71-98 and Nicholas Roe, *John Keats and the Culture of Dissent* (Oxford: Clarendon Press, 1997).
[9] 'I stood tip-toe upon a little hill', *John Keats: Complete Poems,* ed. Jack Stillinger (Cambridge, MA: Belknap Press, 1982) p. 47, lines 23-34.
[10] *The Natural History Prose Writings of John Clare,* ed. Margaret Grainger (Oxford: Clarendon Press, 1983), p. xlviii.
[11] See *The Letters of John Clare,* ed. Mark Storey (Oxford: Clarendon Press, 1985), p. 279, note 5.
[12] Elizabeth Kent, *Flora Domestica; or the Portable Flower-Garden,* (London: Taylor and Hessey, 1823), p. xxi. I also quote this in *John Clare: Love Poems* (Bangkok: M&C Services, 1999), p. x. Through her sister Marianne's marriage to Leigh Hunt, Elizabeth Kent knew Mary and Percy Shelley well. Hunt's attitude to women, and the femininity of flowers, is summed up in his comment in a letter of 1825 to Kent that 'Flora Domestica however is a very pretty appellation for a woman,—one that stays much at home, & hangs her domestic delights with flowers' (*Leigh Hunt: A Life in Letters,* ed. Eleanor M. Gates, Connecticut: Falls River, 1998, p. 167). For other references to Kent see Edmund Blunden, *Leigh Hunt: A Biography* (London: Cobden-Sanderson, 1930), Vol. I of *The Letters of Mary Wollstonecraft Shelley,* ed. Betty T. Bennett (Baltimore: Johns Hopkins UP, 1980) and Molly Tatchell's 'Elizabeth Kent and Flora Domestica', *Keats-Shelley Memorial Bulletin,* 27, (1976), pp. 15-18.
[13] See *By Himself,* eds. Eric Robinson and David Powell (Ashington and Manchester: MidNAG/Carcanet, 1996) p. 188-9. Also Clare's Journal entry for 4th January, 1825:
   the authoress (Miss Kent) of the 'Flora Domestica' says the snow drop is
   the first spring flower   she is mistaken   the yellow winter aconite is
   always earlier and the first on the list of spring (*By Himself,* p. 205).
[14] *Letters of John Clare,* p. 279. This letter of July 1823 was quoted in Taylor and Hessey's *London Magazine* (August 1823, p. 148), without Clare's permission. See *Letters,* p. 279, note 1.
[15] In 1831, Clare wrote to John Taylor:
   & there is Shelly a fine writer & one of the sweetest poems I ever saw was
   of his but I forget it now yet it was somewhere in Benbows Edit of his
   works & it is a long time since I saw them which was at Mrs Emmersons
   (*Letters of John Clare,* p. 545).
The only edition of Shelley's poetry that Clare could be referring to is the piratical *Miscellaneous Poems by Percy Bysshe Shelley* (London: William Benbow, 1826), strangely enough the same edition 'that Robert Browning later picked up on a London bookstall, thus changing his whole life' (Richard Holmes, *Shelley: The Pursuit,* Penguin Books, 1987, p. 209).
[16] Clare snippily wrote in his Journal entry for 14th May 1825: 'a Note also from Miss Kent... to request my assistance to give her information for her intended

History of Birds but if my assistance is not worth more then 12 lines it is worth nothing and I shall not interfere' (*By Himself,* p. 227-8). But he did get a 'very pleasing' and, one can assume, longer, letter in January 1826, and was able to write to Taylor that 'I shall answer it as quickly as possible & give her all the information about birds that I know of for I have abandoned my own intention of writing about them myself as I think she will be able to make a much better work of them then I shoud' (*Letters of John Clare,* pp. 355–6). Kent's bird book never saw publication, but the idea for it may well have been stimulated by Charlotte Smith's successful *The Natural History of Birds; intended chiefly for young persons* (London, 1807).

[17] Alongside 'natural genius' and 'child of nature', the term 'wild flower' was a fairly common label for what we now call a self-taught poet like Clare. For example, Allan Cunningham, a Scottish poet and stonemason who Clare met at *London Magazine* parties in London, had been encouraged to come to the English capital to seek his literary fortune by his editor R. H. Cromek, who wrote in a letter: 'At all events the spring must introduce *you* with other *wild flowers* to the notice of my London friends'; October 27, 1809, quoted in *Poems and Songs by Allan Cunningham,* ed. Peter Cunningham (London: John Murray, 1847), p. xiv-xvi. See also Keats's conception of the young suicidal poet Thomas Chatterton as a 'half-blown flower' in 'Oh Chatterton! how very sad thy fate' (Stillinger, p. 5, line 8), and Samuel Taylor Coleridge's presentation of the same as an 'amaranth, where earth scarce seem'd to own, / Till disappointment came, and pelting wrong / Beat it to earth' in 'On Observing a Blossom on the First of February 1796' (*Poems,* ed. John Beer, London: J. M. Dent, 1993, p. 101, lines 13–15). Clare is not always positive when he compares his own neglected and impoverished situation to that of the wild flower's:
    So like the humble blossom of the field
    Uncultured Genius humble life conceals. ('The humble flower…' p.102)
[18] Edited from Peterborough manuscript A54, p. 2. For the entire introduction and the collection of poetry as Clare designed it, see *The Midsummer Cushion,* eds. Kelsey Thornton and Anne Tibble (Ashington and Manchester: MidNAG/ Carcanet, 1990).
[19] *Love Poems,* ed. Simon Kövesi (Bangkok: M&C Services, 1999), p. 56.
[20] Ronald Blythe, 'Common Pleasures' in *Talking About John Clare* (Nottingham: Trent Books, 1999), p. 136.
[21] Cf.: 'I have no desire further to dry the plant or torture the Butterflye by sticking [it] on a cork board with a pin' (*By Himself,* p. 62) and 'saw a fine Edition of Leniuses Botany with beautiful plates and find that my fern which I found in Harrisons close dyke by the wood lane is the "thorn pointed fern"' (*By Himself,* p. 202). For Darwin, see *Letters of John Clare,* p. 403, note 4.
[22] *The Flora of Northamptonshire,* George Claridge Druce (Arbroath: T. Buncle & Co., 1930), pp. xci, xcvi ff.. In 1955 F. H. Perring added a further 29 species of flower on the basis of new publications, especially *The Letters of John Clare,* eds. J. W. and Anne Tibble (London: Routledge and Kegan Paul, 1951); see F. H.

Perring, 'John Clare and Northamptonshire Plant Records', reprinted from the *Proceedings of the Botanical Society of the British Isles*, Vol. 1, Part 4, October 1955 (Arbroath: T. Buncle & Co. Ltd., 1955).
[23] William Wordsworth, 'Daffodils', line 4 (*Romanticism: An Anthology*, ed. Duncan Wu, Oxford: Blackwell, 2nd ed., 1998, p. 383).
[24] Dorothy Wordsworth, 'The Grasmere Journals', entry for Thursday 15 April 1802' (Duncan Wu, op. cit., p. 434).
[25] '...closer still to Clare in temper is Dorothy Wordsworth in her Grasmere *Journals* (1801–3). Observations of plants, creatures, and the changing seasons are interspersed with unmannered accounts of the doings of the Wordsworth household in a document that is essentially private.' Margaret Grainger, op. cit., p. xlix.
[26] 'Ode to a Nightingale', Stillinger, p. 279–81, line 41: 'I cannot see what flowers are at my feet'.
[27] Blythe, op. cit., p. 134.
[28] Dorothy Wordsworth, 'A Winter's Ramble in Grasmere Vale' (Duncan Wu, op.cit., p.437), lines 17–20 and 29–32. In comparing her vision of the natural world with Clare's, it is interesting to note that she lived in the relatively flat county of Norfolk between the ages of 17 and 23.
[29] See Clare MacDonald Shaw, 'Some Contemporary Women Poets in Clare's Library', *The Independent Spirit: John Clare and the Self-taught Tradition*, ed. John Goodridge (Helpston: John Clare Society, 1994), pp. 87–122.
[30] Charlotte Smith's poetic portraits of flora were no doubt as influential upon Clare as her formal sonnet skills. See Clare MacDonald Shaw, op. cit., p. 116; Judith Pascoe, 'Female Botanists and the Poetry of Charlotte Smith' in *Re-visioning Romanticism: British Women Writers, 1776–1837*, eds. Carol Shiner Wilson and Joel Haefner (Philadelphia: University of Pennsylvania Press, 1994), pp. 193–209; Jacqueline Labbe, 'Every Poet Her Own Master: Charlotte Smith, Anna Seward and *ut pictura poesis*' in *Early Romantics: Perspectives in British Poetry from Pope to Wordsworth*, ed. Thomas Woodman (London: Macmillan, 1998), pp. 200–214. For poetic influences on Clare see Greg Crossan, 'Clare's Debt to the Poets in his Library', *John Clare Society Journal*, 10 (1991), pp. 27–41.
[31] 'Lines Written a Few Miles above Tintern Abbey', (Duncan Wu, op. cit., pp. 265–9) lines 89, 91, 92 respectively.
[32] But Clare does evoke the same Wordsworthian five-year period with 'Five beautiful springs thee and thine have I known' in 'On Some Friends Leaving a Favourite Spot' (below). A major difference from Wordsworth's poem is that Clare uses the passing of five springs to measure his time in Northborough. This is a poem about the annual renewal of Eden.
[33] William H. Galperin uses this term to describe Clare's vision in an extended introductory footnote, in order to *reject* the poet as a subject for his study *The Return of the Visible in British Romanticism* (Baltimore and London: the Johns Hopkins University Press, 1993), note 12, p. 287.

THE PRIMROSE
A SONNET

Welcome pale primrose starting up between
   Dead matted leaves of ash and oak that strew
   The every lawn, the wood and spring through
And creeping moss and joy's darker green;
How much thy presence beautifies the ground,
   How sweet thy modest unaffected pride
   Glows on the sunny bank and wood's warm side,
And when thy fairy flowers in groups are found
   The schoolboy roams enchantedly along,
Plucking the fairest with a rude delight,
   While the meek shepherd stops his simple song
To gaze a moment on the pleasing sight,
   O'erjoyed to see the flowers that truly bring
   The welcome news of sweet returning spring.

TO AN INSIGNIFICANT FLOWER OBSCURELY BLOOMING IN A LONELY WILD

And though thou seemst a weedling wild –
Wild and neglected like to me –
Thou still art dear to nature's child
And I will stoop to notice thee.

For oft like thee, in wild retreat,
Arrayed in humble garb like thee,
There's many a seeming weed proves sweet
As sweet as garden flowers can be.

And like to thee, each seeming weed
Flowers unregarded like to thee –
Without improvement – turns to seed,
Wild and neglected like to me.

Like unto thee, so mean and low,
Nothing boasting like to thee,
No flattering dresses tempting show
Can tempt a friend to notice me.

And like to thee, when beauty's clothed
In lowly raiment like to thee,
Disdaining pride (by beauty loathed)
No beauties there can never see.

For like to thee, my Emma blows;
Flowers like to thee I dearly prize,
And like to thee, her humble clothes
Hides every charm from prouder eyes.

Although like thee, a humble flower
   Is fancied by a polished eye,
It soon should bloom beyond my power
   The finest flower beneath the sky.

And like to thee, loves many a swain
   With genius blest – but like to thee
So humble, lowly, mean and plain,
   No one will notice them, nor me.

So like to thee, they live unknown,
   Wild weeds obscure – and like to thee
Their sweets are sweet to them alone
   – The only pleasure known to me.

Yet when I'm dead let's hope I have
   Some friend in store as I'm to thee,
That will find out my lowly grave
   And heave a sigh to notice me

VIOLET – THOU ART A HOLY BLOSSOM

Violet – thou art a holy blossom,
   In early spring have purpling on my eye,
Most snugly seated in the wood's warm bosom
   Neath budding brambles' sheltering canopy;
Untouched by frowning tempest, howling high
   Their terrors through the oak twigs' melting green
And threatens much the cowslap's trembling flowers;
   Thou ere dwelst peaceful in thy lowly scene,
Thy oaks high-towering and thy hazel bowers,
   Thou lowly hermit flower of solitude,
Thou plainly tellst a lesson unto me;
   The naked hill bears all the tempest rude,
That wind descends to touch such thing as thee.

TO THE VIOLET

Hail to the violet! Sweet careless spread
  Neath each warm bush and covert budding hedge,
In many a pleasing walk have I been led
  To seek thee – promise of spring's earliest pledge –
In modest coyness hanging down its head,
  Unconscious hiding beauties from the eye
And sweetly brooding o'er its graceful form,
  Shunning each vulgar gaze that saunters by
And tim'ly stooping from an April storm;
  As virtue startled by approaching harm
Shrinks from delusion's false betraying hand
  With bashful look that more the bosom warms,
So sweetest blossom the coy violet stands
  Tempting the plunderer with a double charm.

TO A COWSLIP EARLY

Cowslip bud so early peeping
   Warmed by April's hazard hours,
O'er thy head though sunshine's creeping
   'Hind it threatened tempests lower;
Trembling blossom let me bear thee
   To a better, safer home,
Though a fairer blossom wear thee
   Ne'er a tempest there shall come.

Mary's bonny breasts to charm thee
   Bosom soft as down can be,
Eyes like any suns to warm thee
   And scores of sweets unknown to me;
Ah for joys thou'lt there be meeting
   In a station so divine,
I'd most wish that's vain repeating,
   Cowslip bud thy life were mine.

SONNET
TO A RED CLOVER BLOSSOM

Sweet bottle-shaped flower of lushy red,
   Born when the summer wakes her warmest breeze
Among the meadows waving grasses spread,
   Or neath the shade of hedge or clumping trees,
Bowing on slender stem thy heavy head;
In sweet delight I view thy summer bed
   And hark the drone of heavy humble bees
Along thy honeyed garden led,
   Down cornfield-striped baulks and pasture leas –
Fond warmings of the soul that long has fled
   Revives my bosom wi' their sweetness still,
As I bend myself o'er thy ruddy pride
   Recalling days I dropped upon a hill
And cut my oaten trumpets by thy side.

BALLAD

A weedling wild on lonely lea
My evening rambles chanced to see,
And much the weedling tempted me
   To crop its tender flower;
Exposed to wind and heavy rain
Its head bowed lowly on the plain,
And silently it seemed complain
   Of life's endangered hour.

And wild thou bid my bloom decay
And crop my flower and me betray
And cast my injured sweets away,
   Its silence seemly sighed;
A moment's idol of thy mind
And is a stranger so unkind
To leave a shameful root behind
   Bereft of all its pride.

And so it seemly did complain
And beating fell the heavy rain,
And low it drooped upon the plain
   To fate resigned to fall;
My heart did melt at its decline
'And come,' said I, 'thou gem divine,
My fate shall stand the storm wi' thine,'
   So took the root and all.

THE HUMBLE FLOWER THAT BUDS UPON THE PLAIN

The humble flower that buds upon the plain
And only buds to blossom but in vain,
   By senseless rustics with unheeding eyes
   Still trodden down as they attempt to rise,

So like the humble blossom of the field,
Uncultured Genius humble life conceals.

SONG

Swamps of wild rush beds and slough's squashy traces,
    Grounds of rough fallows wi' thistle and weed,
Flats and low valleys of kingcups and daisies,
    Sweetest of subjects are ye for my reed;
Ye commons left free in the rude rags of nature,
    Ye brown heaths beclothed in furze as ye be,
My wild eye in rapture adores e'ery feature;
    Ye're as dear as this heart in my bosom to me.

O native endearments I would not forsake ye,
    I would not forsake ye for sweetest of scenes,
For sweetest of gardens that nature could make me,
    I would not forsake ye dear valleys and greens;
Though nature ne'er dropped thee a cloud-resting mountain
    Nor waterfalls tumble their music to thee,
Had nature denied thee a bush, tree or fountain,
    Thou still would' bin loved as an Eden by me.

And long my dear valleys long, long may ye flourish,
    Though rush beds and thistles make most of your pride,
May showers never fail the green daisies to nourish,
    Nor suns dry the fountain that rills by its side;
Yer skies may be gloomy and misty yer mornings,
    Yer flat swampy valleys unwholesome may be,
Still refuse of nature wi'out her adornings
    Ye're as dear as this heart in my bosom to me.

THRICE WELCOME SWEET SUMMER IN SOFTNESS RETURNING

Thrice welcome sweet summer in softness returning,
   Thrice welcome ye skies wi' no clouds on your brow;
Again ye return my delight of the morning
   My love's on the pasture a-milking her cow.

Thrice welcome ye flowers I rejoice in your blooming,
   Ye cowslaps dew–shaken by night-roving cow;
And eglantine brambles of sweetest perfuming,
   I'll rub off your weapons a wreath for her brow.

O welcome ye 'awthorns, your green leaves delight me,
   O'er arching the brook wi' your thick screening bough;
In your secret shelter shall kisses requite me,
   As I bear home the pail of my love from her cow.

O NATIVE SCENES, NOUGHT TO MY HEART CLINGS NEARER

O native scenes, nought to my heart clings nearer
    Than you ye dews of my youthful hours;
Nought in this world warms my affections dearer
    Than you ye plains of 'white and yellow flowers',
Than you ye 'awthorns' shades and woodbines' bowers,
    Where youth had roved and still where manhood roves
The pasture pathway neath its willow groves;
    O as my eye looks on your lovely scenes
All, all those joys of former life beholding,
    'Spite of the pain, the care, that intervenes,
When loved remembrance is her bliss unfolding,
    Picking her childish posies on your greens,
My soul can peer o'er its distress awhile,
And sorrow's cheek finds leisure for a smile.

A WILD NOSEGAY

The yellow lambtoe I have often got
   Sweet-creeping o'er the banks in summertime,
And totter-grass in many a trembling knot
   And robbed the molehill of its bed of thyme;
And oft wi' anxious feelings would I climb
   The waving willow row, a stick to trim,
To search the water lily's tempting flowers
   That on the surface then did tempting swim;
I've stretched and tried vain schemes for many an hour
   And scrambled up the 'awthorn's prickly bower
For ramping woodbines and blue bittersweet,
   Still summer blooms these flowers have conned again;
But ah the question's useless to repeat –
   When will the feelings come I witnessed then?

THERE'S THE DAISY, THE WOODBINE

There's the daisy, the woodbine
   And crowflower so golden;
There's the wild rose, the eglantine
   And may buds unfolding;
There's flowers for my fairy,
   There's bowers for my love,
Wilt thou gang wi' me Mary
   To the banks of Brooms-grove.

There's the thorn bush and the ashen tree
   For to shield from the heat,
While the brook for refreshing thee
   Runs close by thy feet;
The thrushes is chanting dear
   Mid the pleasures of love,
Thou'rt the only thing wanted here
   Mid the sweets of Brooms-grove.

Then come ere a minute's gone
   In the long summer's day,
Puts her wings swift as linnet's on,
   For hieing away;
Then come wi' no doubts near
   To fear a false love,
For there's nothing wi' out thee dear
   Can please in Brooms-grove.

The woodbine may nauntle dear
   In blossoms so fine,
The wild rose mantle near
   In blushes may shine;
Mary queen of each blossom proves
   She's the blossom I love,
She's the all that my bosom loves
   'Mong the sweets of Brooms-grove.

ON SOME FRIENDS LEAVING A FAVOURITE SPOT

Though thou wert not the place of my being and birth
   Though I spent not the sports of my childhood in thee,
Yet amid the dear spots we call Edens on earth
   Thou art one of the fairest that's known unto me;
Five beautiful springs thee and thine have I known,
   Thy woods and thy brooks winding peaceful at will,
Thy heaths and like hermitage standing alone
   Thy cottage that smokes by the side of a hill.

I have rambled thy plains where no being beside
   Hath intruded the length of a whole summer's day
And followed the shepherd's path dimly descried
   By the hedges all lined wi' dog-roses and may
And wilds where no tracks but the rabbits hath been,
   Where flowers bloom untouched till they fade seed and die,
Where the whole summer through ne'er a school boy is seen
   And the linnet's brood lives in their nest till they fly.

I have turned to thy springs with the birds when a-dry,
   And hunted thy flowers with the hoarse humming bee,
And the few scantling pleasures that manhood supply
   Were some of them sought for and gathered in thee;
And a flower that grew with thee, the fairest of all,
   That decks the soft bosom of April and May,
Blooming lovely and wild by the lone cottage wall
   Love wooed it with rapture and won it away.

And I've walked o'er thy wilds with the flower I esteem
   And lived in the peace of her cottage a guest,
And mused o'er the charms of thy heath and thy stream
   As she sunk in our walks on my bosom to rest;
And the bowers on thy heaths sprinkled o'er with cows
   Where we met down at noon, a cool minute to spend,
Enjoying the breeze that fanned through the green boughs,
   When I left them I bade 'em farewell like a friend.

Where the brook from its fountain rock drop after drop
　　Muttered lonely and hid on its half-buried way,
Where shades on each side grew and met at the top
　　And made it seem night in the midst of the day;
The dove hid her there where its foes rarely pass
　　Far away from the haunts of the rude netterd boy,
And the brown bee its honey herds in the tall grass
　　Where the mower ne'er comes with a scythe to destroy.

Though spring brings the wild heath its annual bloom
　　Spreading white sheets of flowers on the thorns dripping bough,
Yet tyrants have been with the friends of her home
　　And strangers are there to inhabit it now;
The footpath as usual inviteth us on,
　　And the old cottage still peeps o'er the dell,
But the friends of the blossom I gathered are gone
　　And bidden the fields and the dwelling farewell.

We might roam as wont to the heath's yellow o'er
　　With furze flowers and lambtoe thick-creeping and rove
Down the crooked path that leads to the fountain once more;
　　The scenes of her childhood and haunts of our love
And the cottage would shine just the same in her eye,
　　But the voice of old welcomes would meet us no more,
We might pass her loved dwelling as strangers pass by,
　　And no eye would notice or open the door.

I loved the dear haunts and the sweet solitudes
　　That round its lone walls in the circle did lie,
Where no living thing all the season intrudes
　　But a bird or a bee humming wearisome by;
And I've hunted for spots by the brook and have found
　　The loneliest existing an hour to abide,
With nought but the green light of trees flitting round
　　And the shadow that seemed stretched asleep by my side.

The wood rides as wont wind beneath the oak bough
   Still tempting the eye that admires to rove on,
But stranger feet walk in their lowliness now
   And their old fellow hermits that loved them are gone;
The buds in the garden shades nestling among
   As fond of their neighbours that used to dwell by,
Hear strange voices now and stop short in their song
   And startled peep down on fresh faces and fly.

The sparrows no doubt will grow coy and complain
   To meddlesome foes that their freedom is gone,
And the fond robin pause ere he ventures again
   To pick up the crumbles of bread by the door;
The martin that yet to the cottage repairs
   That once met a welcome and quiet enjoyed,
May now find a tyrant as cruel as theirs
   And mourning retreat from its dwelling destroyed.

The black bee that hums by the mud-creviced wall
   Even they may old friends and old neighbours deplore,
While meddlesome children in frolicsome brawl
   Shouteth loudly that friendship and freedom is o'er;
I've seen these delights in their season of peace
   When their old friends and neighbours was labouring nigh,
Ere a tyrant's intrusions had warned them to cease,
   And I deeply regret that such seasons are by.

Long, long in seclusion their lives had been nursed,
   Neighbours only to blossoms to birds and to bees,
Till plum stones and damsons set when they came first
   And small apple kernels had grown up to trees,
And a thorn that was not when they came to the spot
   Which a linnet might bring when an 'aw from the dell
Had grown when they left half as high as the cot,
   And quite overshadowed the curb of the well.

The woodbine that crept up the door and peeped in
   May with them of its bloom and its home be bereft,
That cling to the cot with its inmates akin,
   And they felt that it viewed them as such when they left,
When they left birds and flowers, all their neighbours, behind,
   In the noise and the strife of a village to dwell,
They seemed to have borrowed the voice of the wind,
   And to sigh when their last look turned on them 'farewell'.

FAIRY ELVES, THOSE MINUTE THINGS

Fairy elves, those minute things
   That sleep and dream in flowers,
That come on summer's golden wings
   To dance in moonlight bowers;
That on a mushroom table sups
   By glow-worm's trembling light,
And drink their dews from acorn cups
   Through summer's pleasant night.

A WALK

The thorn tree just began to bud
   And greening stained the sheltering hedge,
And many a vi'let 'side the wood
   Peeped blue between the withered sedge;
The sun gleamed warm the bank beside,
   'Twas pleasant wandering out awhile
Neath nestling bush to lonely hide,
   Or bend in musings o'er a stile.

I wandered down the narrow lane
   Whose battered paths was hardly dry,
And to the wild heath went again
   Upon its wilderness to lie;
There mixed wi' joy that never tires
   Far from the busy hum of men,
Among its molehills, furze and briars
   Then further strolled and dropped again.

MILD HEALTH I SEEK THEE, WHITHER ART THOU FOUND?

Mild health I seek thee, whither art thou found?
Mid daisies sleeping in the morning dew,
Along the meadow paths where all around
   May smells so lovely, thither would I go;
Where art thou envious blessing? Now the cold
   Is gone away and hedge and wood is seen
All lovely and the gay marsh marigold
   Edges the meadow lakes so freshly green,
My straining eye so anxious to behold
   Thee up and journeying on the swallow's wing,
To see thee up and shining everywhere
   Among the sweet companions of the spring.

THE DAISY WAN, THE PRIMROSE PALE

The daisy wan, the primrose pale,
   Seem nought but white and yellow flowers
To every heedless passer-by,
   When they attend the spring's young hours;
But they are loves and friends to me
   That tell me each in short sojourn
Of what they felt and I did feel
   In springs that never will return.

CHILDHOOD

The past it is a magic word
   Too beautiful to last;
It looks back like a lovely face
   Who hath not felt the past;
There's music in its childhood
   That's known in every tongue,
Like the music of the wild wood
   All chorus to the song.

The happy dream, the joyous play,
   The life without a sigh,
The beauty thoughts can ne'er portray
   In those four letters lie;
The painter's beauty, breathing arts,
   The poet's speaking pens,
Can ne'er call back a thousand part
   Of what that word contains.

And fancy at its sweetest hour,
   What e'er may come to pass,
Shall find that magic thrill no more:
   Time broke it like his glass;
The sweetest joy, the fairest face
   The treasure most preferred,
Have left the honours of their place
   Locked in that silent word.

When we look back on what we were
   And feel what we are now,
A fading leaf is not so drear
   Upon a broken bough;
A winter seat without a fire,
   A cold world without friends,
Doth not such chilly glooms impart
   As that one word portends.

Like withered wreaths in banquet halls
   When all the rout is past,
Like sunshine that on ruins falls
   Our pleasures are at last;
The joy is fled, the love is cold
   And beauty's splendour too,
Our first believings - all are old
   And faith itself untrue.

When beauty met love's budding spring
   In artless witcheries,
It were not then an earthly thing
   But an angel in disguise;
Where are they now of youth's esteems?
   All shadows past away;
Flowers blooming but in summer dreams
   And thoughts of yesterday

Our childhood soon a trifle gets
   Yet like a broken toy,
Grown out of date it recollects
   Our memories into joy;
The simple catalogue of things
   That reason would despise,
Starts in the head a thousand springs
   Of half-forgotten joys.

When we review that place of prime
   That childhood's joys endow,
That seemed more green in winter time
   Than summer grass does now;
Where oft the task of skill was put
   For other boys to match,
To run along the churchyard wall
   Or bouncing balls to catch.

How oft we clomb the porch to cut
   Our names upon the leads,
Though fame nor any thing akin
   Was never in our heads;
Where hands and feet were rudely drawn
   And names we could not spell,
And thought no artist in the world
   Could ever do as well.

We twirled our tops that spun so well
   They scarce could tumble down,
And thought they twirled as well again
   When riddled on the crown;
And bee-spell marbles bound to win
   As by a potent charm,
Was often wetted in the mouth
   To show the dotted swarm.

We pelted at the weather cock
   And he who pelted o'er
Was reckoned as a mighty man
   And ever something more;
We leapt across 'cat gallow sticks'
   And mighty proud was he
Who overshot the famous nicks
   That reached above his knee.

And then each other's tasks we did
   And great ambition grew;
We ran so swift - so strong we leaped
   We almost thought we flew;
We saw across the broken brig
   Whose wooden rail was lost
And loud the victor's feat was hailed
   Who dared the danger most.

And hopscotch too - a spur to joy -
   We thought the task divine
To hop and kick the stone right out
   And never touch a line;
And then we walked on mighty stilts
   Scarce seven inches high,
Yet on we stalked and thought ourselves
   Already at the sky.

Our pride to reason would not shrink
   In these exalted hours,
A giant's was a pigmy link
   To statures such as ours;
We even fancied we could fly
   And fancy then was true,
So with the clouds upon the sky
   In dreams at night we flew.

We shot our arrows from our bows
   Like any archers proud,
And thought when lost they went so high
   To lodge upon a cloud;
And these seemed feats that none before
   Ourselves could e'er attain,
And Wellington with all his feats
   Felt never half so vain.

Soft we urged the barking dog -
   For mischief was our glee -
To chase the cat up weed-green walls
   And mossy apple tree;
When her tail stood like a bottle brush
   With fear - we laughed again;
Like tyrants we could purchase mirth
   And ne'er allow for pain.

And then our play pots sought and won
   For uses and for show,
That Wedgwood's self with all his skill
   Might guess in vain to know;
And palaces of stone and stick
   In which we could not creep,
Which Nash himself ne'er made so quick
   And never half so cheap.

Our fancies made us great and rich -
   No bounds our wealth could fix:
A stool drawn round the room was soon
   A splendid coach and six;
The magic of our minds was great,
   And even pebbles they
Soon as we chose to call them gold
   Grew guineas in our play.

And carriages of oyster shells
   Though filled with nought but stones,
Grew instant ministers of state
   While clay kings filled their thrones;
Like Cinderella's fairy queen
   Joy would our wants bewitch;
If wealth was sought the dust and stones
   Turned wealth and made us rich.

The mallow seed became a cheese,
   The henbanes loaves of bread,
A burdock leaf our tablecloth
   On a table stone was spread;
The bindweed flower that climbs the hedge
   Made us a drinking glass,
And these we spread our 'Mayor's feast'
   Upon the summer grass.

A henbane root could scarcely grow,
    A mallow shake its seeds,
The insects that might feed thereon
    Found famine in the weeds;
But like the pomp of princely taste
    That humbler life annoys,
We thought not of our neighbour's wants
    While we were wasting joys.

We often tried to force the snail
    To leave his harvest hour,
By singing that the beggar man
    Was coming for his corn;
We thought we forced the lady-cow
    To tell the time of day,
'Twas one o'clock and two o'clock
    And then she flew away.

We bawled to beetles as they ran
    That their children were all gone,
Their houses down and door key hid
    Beneath the golden stone;
They seemed to haste as fast again
    While we shouted as they past,
With mirth half-mad to think our tale
    Had urged their speed so fast.

The stonecrop that on ruins comes
    And hangs like golden balls,
How oft to reach its shining blooms
    We scaled the mossy walls;
And weeds – we gathered weeds as well
    Of all that bore a flower,
And tied our little posies up
    Beneath the eldern bower.

Our little gardens there we made
   Of blossoms all a-row,
And though they had no roots at all
   We hoped to see them grow;
And in the cart rut after showers
   Of sudden summer rain,
We filled our tiny water pots
   And cherished them in vain.

We pulled the moss from apple trees
   And gathered bits of straws,
When weary twirling of our tops
   And shooting of our taws;
We made birds' nests and thought that birds
   Would like them ready-made,
And went full twenty times a day
   To see if eggs were laid.

The long and swaily willow row
   Where we for whips would climb,
How sweet their shadows used to grow
   In merry harvest time;
We pulled boughs down and made a swee
   Snug hid from toil and sun,
And up we tossed right merrily
   Till weary with the fun.

On summer eves with wild delight
   We bawled the bat to spy,
Who in the 'I spy' dusky light
   Shrieked loud and flickered by;
And up we knocked our shuttlecocks
   And tried to hit the moon,
And wondered bats should fly so long
   And they come down so soon.

We sought for nuts in secret nook
    We thought none else could find,
And listened to the laughing brook
    And mocked the singing wind;
We gathered acorns ripe and brown
    That hung too high to pull,
Which friendly winds would shake a-down
    Till all had pockets full.

Then loading home at day's decline
    Each sought his corner stool
Then went to bed till morning came
    And crept again to school;
Yet there by pleasure unforsook
    In nature's happy moods:
The cuts in 'Fenning's Spelling Book'
    Made up for fields and woods.

Each noise that breathed around us then
    Was magical and song
Wherever pastime found us then
    Joy never led us wrong;
The wild bee in the blossom hung
    The coy bird's startled call
To find its home in danger – there
    Was music in them all.

And o'er the first bumbarrel's nest
    We wondered at the spell
That birds who served no 'prenticeship
    Could build their nests so well;
And finding linnet's moss was green
    And buntings chusing grey
And every bunting's nest alike
    Our wits was all away.

Then blackbirds lining theirs with grass
    And thrushes theirs with dung,
So for our lives we could not tell
    From whence the wisdom sprung;
We marvelled much how little birds
    Should ever be so wise
And so we guessed some angel came
    To teach them from the skies.

In winter too we traced the fields
    And still felt summer joys;
We sought our hips and felt no cold:
    Cold never came to boys;
The sloes appeared as choice as plums
    When bitten by the frost
And crabs grew honey in the mouth
    When apple time was past.

We rolled in sunshine lumps of snow
    And called them mighty men
And tired of pelting Bonneparte
    We ran to slide again;
And ponds for glibbest ice we sought
    With shouting and delights
And tasks of spelling all were left
    To get by heart at night.

And when it came – and round the fire
    We sat – what joy was there!
The kitten dancing round the cork
    That dangled from a chain,
While we our scraps of paper burnt
    To watch the flitting sparks
And Collect books were often torn
    For parsons and for clerks.

Nought seemed too hard for us to do
   But the sums upon our slates;
Nought seemed too high for us to win
   But the Master's chair of state;
The 'Town of Troy' we tried and made
   When our sums we could not try
While we envied e'en the sparrow's wings
   From our prison house to fly.

When twelve o'clock was counted out
   The joy and strife began:
The shut of books, the hearty shout
   As out of doors we ran;
Sunshine and showers, who could withstand
   Our food and rapture they;
We took our dinners in our hands
   To lose no time in play.

The morn when first we went to school
   Who can forget the morn
When the birch whip lay upon the clock
   And our hornbook it was torn;
We tore the little pictures out,
   Less fond of books than play,
And only took one letter home
   And that the letter 'A'.

I love in childhood's little book
   To read its lessons through
And o'er each pictured page to look
   Because they read so true;
And there my heart creates anew
   Love for each trifling thing
– Who can disdain the meanest weed
   That shows its face at spring?

The daisy looks up in my face
   As long ago it smiled:
It knows no change but keeps its place
   And takes me for a child;
The bunting in the hedgerow thorn
   Cries 'pink pink pink' to hear
My footsteps in the early morn
   As though a boy was near.

I seek no more the bunting's nest
   Nor stoop for daisy flowers;
I grow a stranger to myself
   In these delightful hours;
Yet when I hear the voice of spring
   I can but call to mind
The pleasures which they used to bring,
   The joys I used to find.

The firetail on the orchard wall
   Keeps at its startled cry
Of 'tweet tut tut' nor sees the morn
   Of boyhood's mischief by;
It knows no change of changing time,
   By sickness never stung,
It feeds on hope's eternal prime
   Around its brooded young.

Ponds where we played at 'Duck and Drake'
   Where the ash with ivy grew,
Where we robbed the owl of all her eggs
   And mocked her as she flew;
The broad tree in the spinney hedge
   'Neath which the gypsies lay
Where we our fine oak apples got
   On the twenty-ninth of May.

These all remain as then they were
   And are not changed a day
And the ivy's crowns as near to green
   As mine is to the grey;
It shades the pond, o'erhangs the stile,
   And the oak is in the glen
But the paths to joy are so worn out
   I can't find one again.

The merry wind still sings the song
   As if no change had been;
The birds build nests the summer long
   And trees look full as green
As e'er they did in childhood's joy
   Though they hath long been by
When I, a happy roving boy,
   In the fields had used to lie

To tend the restless roving sheep
   Or lead the quiet cow:
Toils that seemed more than slavery then
   How more than freedom now;
Could we but feel as then we did
   When joy too fond to fly
Would flutter round as soon as bid
   And drive all troubles by.

But rainbows on an April cloud
   And blossoms plucked in May
And painted eves that summer brings
   Fade not so fast away;
Though grass is green, though flowers are gay
   And everywhere they be,
What are the leaves on branches hung
   Unto the withered tree?

Life's happiest gifts and what are they?
   Pearls by the morning strung
Which ere the morn are swept away
   – Short as a cuckoo's song,
A nightingale's, the summer is;
   Can pleasure make us proud
To think when swallows fly away
   They leave her in her shroud?

Youth revels at his rising hour
   With more than summer joys
And rapture holds the fairy flower
   Which reason soon destroys;
O sweet the bliss which fancy feigns
   To hide the eyes of truth
And beauteous still the chain appears
   Of faces loved in youth.

And spring returns the blooming year
   Just as it used to be
And joys in youthful smiles appear
   To mock the change in me;
Each night leaves memory ill at ease
   And stirs an aching bosom
To think that seasons sweet as these
   With me are out of blossom.

The fairest summer sinks in shade
   The sweetest blossom dies
And age finds every beauty fade
   That youth esteemed a prize;
The play breaks up the blossom fades
   And childhood disappears
For higher dooms ambition aims
   And care grows into years.

But time we often blame him wrong
    That rude destroying time
And follow him with sorrow's song
    When he hath done no crime;
Our joys in youth are often sold
    In folly's thoughtless fray
And many feel their hearts grow old
    Before their heads are grey.

The past there lies in that one word
    Joys more than wealth can crown,
Nor could a million call them back
    Though muses wrote them down;
The sweetest joys imagined yet,
    The beauties that impressed,
All life or fancy ever met
    Are there among the past.

THE ANNIVERSARY
TO A FLOWER OF THE DESERT

March wakened in wildness
   Or musing in glee
Thy tempest or sunshine
   Is welcome to me;
I found on thy bosom
   A treasure of spring
A fairer and dearer
   Than summer could bring.

Ere the throstle had ventured
   A song to the morn
Or the blackbird to build him
   A nest in the thorn,
On the wild hills of Walk'erd
   All witherd and bare,
Had Eden existed
   I had thought it was there.

Hope long had been blighted
   Love lingered in chains
Faith long had been plighted
   To scorn and disdains;
The road it was weary
   That led me along
With no thought to cheer me
   But the sorrows of song.

I looked to the east 'twas
   A sunrise in shrouds,
I looked to the west there
   Was nothing but clouds;
In aching and sorrow
   Hope had lost her employ,
She had grief for the morrow
   But no day for joy.

Here a sunburst a cloud where
  I looked for a shower;
Here a spot that seemed desert
  Discovered a flower;
Endowed in youth's glory
  Both blossom and stem
Was the model of beauty
  And I worshiped the gem.

For my heart it was neuter
  To form and disguise
Nor like a freebooter
  I looked on the prize;
But with heart that felt friendless
  And wanted a friend,
On a way that seemed endless
  And now met an end.

I loved it and proved it
  And down to this hour
I ne'er saw the beauty
  I found in that flower;
Summer lived in its blossom
  The winter was by,
Joy laughed on its bosom
  Though winter was nigh.

A palace without it
  A prison would be
And the cottage that owned it
  Was a palace to me;
My heart it was weary
  I sued as a guest,
Love was all that could cheer me
  And there I had rest.

THE HOLIDAY WALK

Come Eliza and Anna lay by top and ball
And friendly boy throw away cart and toys all,
   Look about for your hats and dispense with your play
   We'll seek for the fields and be happy today;
Do but hark at the shouts of the boys by the school
As noisy and merry as geese in a pool,
   While the Master himself is so sick of his thrall
   That he laughs like the merriest child of them all:
While they race with their shadows he joins in the play
And leaps o'er the 'cat gallows' nimble as they,
   As glad to get out of his school in the sun
   As a captive would be from his prison to run.
The morning invites us to walk, come along,
'Tis so sweet that the sparrow e'en tries at a song;
   The dews are all gone save amid the dark glooms
   Neath the wood's crowded leaves where the sun never comes,
Nor need we regret that the dews linger there
For brambles defy us to come if we dare,
   And doubtless each poor little bird in the end
   Is glad to consider the bramble its friend,
For girls even often its dwelling destroys
And boys are so cruel, birds cannot like boys.
   So we'll be contented to roam far away
   Through bean fields in blossom and closes of hay;
Do but look at those ducks, how delighted they seem
All plashing and cleaning themselves in the stream
   And the swallow that loves in black chimneys to sing
   Will scarcely dart o'er without washing his wing.
Now we're out of the town see the fields how they smile
So sweet that the boy climbs astride on the stile
   To gaze round about him as much as to say
   'I should like to go where it pleased me today';
But poor little fellow he wishes in spite
Of his toil – for his sheep they want tending till night.

Look here as we come in this cool narrow lane
How close martins pass us and pass us again,
Darting on by the side of the hedges they go
As swift as an arrow shot out of a bow.
    The dust is all past which we met in the street
    And the grass like a carpet spreads under our feet;
See there's a fine butterfly sits on that leaf,
Aye you may go creeping as still as a thief,
    It can hear you and see you – see there up it flies
    With wings like the rainbow you've seen in the skies
Yes! Yes, you may run, there it crosses the stream
As far out of reach as a joy in a dream.
    Aye now it delights ye to look at the sky:
    Those are hawks sailing proud as the clouds and as high,
See there one's at rest hanging still even now
As fixed in the air as a bird on a bough;
    These are sweet sights in sooth but the milking maid sees
    The sky every morning near sweeter than these,
When she hies to her cows while the sun large and round
Starts up like a table of fire from the ground,
    And she sees it so often she gives it no praise
    Though some never saw it, not once all their days.
This morning I marked in what splendour he rose
Like a king of the east ere his journey he goes;
    His bed in the skies any fancy might trace
    With a curtain of scarlet half hiding her face,
Then as he rose up to his throne for a seat
It changed to a carpet of gold at his feet,
    Then as a magician's wand touched it there came
    A dye o'er the east of all hues ye can name:
A dappled profusion of gold, blue and red,
Like pavements of rubies where angels may tread,
    A shadow e'en now of its splendour remains
    Like an old ruined tapestry all blotches and stains
Giving lessons of grandeur and earthly parade;

To think even heaven hath glories that fade
   Nay sigh not at all, you shall see by and by
   The sun rise as oft as the milkmaid and I.
Stop! There's a wasps' nest, what a bustle and hum
Like legions of armies where danger is come,
   There they rush one by one in their jackets of yellow
   Not one offers fight but he's backed by his fellow,
So come on nor search at that rose on the bower,
We'll hazard no wounds for the sake of a flower.
   Here's the snail with his fine painted shell at his back
   And there's one without in his jacket of black,
The path's even covered with insects – each sort
Flock by crowds in the smiles of the morning to sport;
   There's the cricket in brown and his cousin in green
   The grasshopper dancing and o'er them is seen
The ladybird dressed like a hunter in red
Creeping out from the blossoms with whom she went bed.
   So good little girls now disturb not their play
   And you Freddy stop till they hop far away,
For to kill them in sport as a many folks will
And call it a pastime 'tis cruel and ill,
   As their lives are as sweet of enjoyment as ours
   And they dote like yourselves upon sunshine and flowers.
See yonder's some boys all at swee in the cool
On the wood-riding gate playing truant from school;
   How gladly they seek the field's freedom to play
   To swee creaking gates and to roll in the hay,
Mocking loud the wood echoes that answer again
In musical 'haloos' so soft and so plain,
   That they no longer dread them as giants or elves
   But think them all boys fond of sport as themselves,
And they shout in their pastimes to coax them away
From the wood's gloomy arbours to join in their play.
   Now loves ye are weary I see by your walk
   Well well here's a sweet cock of hay on the baulk;

An ash hung with ivy too leans from the stile
So sit you down here and we'll rest us awhile,
   But not on that molehill for see what a mass
   Of pismires are nimbling about in the grass;
If you had crumbs to throw them they'd haul them away
And never seem weary the whole summer's day,
   And if you sit on them as small as they are
   They'll sting you and tease you so prithee beware!
Do but look how the fields slope away from our eyes
Till the trees in the distance seem clouds in the skies,
   A map spreads about us in green of all stains
   Dark woods, paler meadows and fields' varied grains
And look o'er the gap of yon hedge and behold
Yon turnip lands seeming as littered with gold,
   'Tis the charlock in blossom, a troublesome weed,
   Yet a beautiful sight in the distance indeed;
They are nought for a nosegay yet still in fine weather
You see what a show they make growing together.
   Aye yonder are steeples that catch on the eye
   Like giants of stone stretching up the blue sky,
And windmills are sweeping their sails up and down
And cottages peeping all sunny and brown,
   See the cows grazing yonder and less quiet sheep,
   Some at feed and some chewing their cuds till they sleep;
Thus the prospect in varied profusions abound
And spreadeth a beautiful picture around,
   Though there shines no old ruins for artists to prize
   Nor mountains to thrust up their heads to the skies,
Yet as like De Wint's pictures as nature can be
For nature owns no sweeter painter than he.
   Nay don't be alarmed and start up from the hay,
   That's nought but a little mouse running away
And now she finds out we're not foes to destroy
Do but hear in the grass how she chitters for joy;
   No doubt in the beans night at hand may sojourn
   Her children awaiting her mother's return.

See there where the willow bends over the brook
At our feet like an old shepherd over his crook,
   Neath its boughs gnats and midges are still at their play
   Like ballrooms of fairies all dancing away;
Aye there in rich dress goes the great dragonfly
Like another proud thing buzzing scornfully by,
   He scarce turns his head on their dancing and glee
   And they're full as careless of notice as he.
O don't you, my Anna, be cruel and vain,
The smallest of things are not strangers to pain:
   That long legged shepherd you've caught, let him go!
   For he knows naught at all what you threaten no, no!
Though you tell him you'll kill both his son and his daughter
If he will not afford you a small drop of water,
   Your threats and your language he can't understand
   Though he sheds tears for freedom while shut in your hand.
And here's little Freddy crying 'click clocking clay'
Poh! Ladybirds know not the time of the day,
   Of 'one o clock, two o clock', no such a thing,
   So give it its freedom and let it take wing.
Well now, if you're rested we'll wander again:
Here the path strides the brook over closes of grain,
   So who's first to venture? Come never see fear,
   Though the plank bends beneath no danger is near;
Well if you are fearful we'll turn back and go
Where stepping stones ford o'er a shallow below;
   Danger's seldom, my children, so near as we think
   And often seems far when we stand on the brink,
As the runlet in shallows bawls loud and in deeps
Deceitfully sinks into silence and sleeps.
   Do but try how delicious those bean blossoms smell,
   No flower in the garden delights me so well,
Perfuming the nest of the partridge that lies
Basking safe in the shadows their forest supplies,
   And the hare: here's a beaten path tracks her retreat
   Feels timidly safe in her corn-covered seat

On this mown baulk, no doubt she oft ventures to play
When a grasshopper's rustle might fright her away.
   How sweet and how happy such places appear,
   Well indeed may you wish that our cottage was here,
With the wild bees for neighbours the whole summer long
And the lark ever near us a-piping his song,
   With the beans in full blossom close up to our door
   And cows in the distance at feed on the moor
And grasshoppers singing where'er we might roam
And partridges calling at night by our home;
   Where we might sit at eve in our parlour and see
   The rabbit bob out from that old hollow tree,
And hear from yon thicket so gloomy and deep
The sweet little nightingale sing us to sleep
   Which we heard t'other night – don't you recollect now?
   When I clomb the wood stile to get each one a bough,
How one sung 'jug jug' and you all sung amain
'Jug jug' and laughed loud as it answered again.
   Aye aye, I knew well such a beautiful song
   Would not be so quickly forgot, come along,
For the day gets so hot you may well wish again
To meet with the coolness we left in the lane.
   Do but look at our shadows: what strangers we've got;
   Those giants that came with us first from our cot,
Stalking on stride for stride in a pomp-stirring mood
Nigh as tall as the oaks that lay peeled by the wood,
   Whose long legs might cross a brook ever so wide
   And leap o'er a hedge, nay a house, at a stride;
They've left us and shrunk from our sight by degrees
To children and dwarfs scarce as high as our knees
   That as we go on shrink so close to our feet
   As if they were glad to get out of the heat.
Come here is the footpath that leads to the town
Don't stop – 'tis so hot loves – we cannot sit down.
   O I see what delights ye – aye climb on the stile
   And look round about as ye wish for a while.

Those things that go sweeing away to the wind
Though the willows scarce move that are growing behind
   Are the sails of the Mill – and indeed as you say
   They follow each other like things in their play,
Now dropping then rising their wearisome round
And seem where you stand to spring out of the ground;
   Yon shepherd boy doubtless thinks so as he lies
   Lolling o'er the gate gazing in happy surprise.
See now they move slower, the wind's nearly still
And there comes the miller – look – out of his mill
   To peep at the weather with meal powdered o'er,
   More white than the dog-rose in bloom by the door.
See there goes the mower a-sweeping away
And yon folks in the nook, see, are stacking of hay,
   Some loading, some forking, the grounds are alive
   With their labour, as busy as bees in a hive.
There's no one seems idle but this little boy
Who runs after butterflies bawling for joy,
   And now he has run like a fox in the wheat
   (If the farmer came by he would surely get beat)
The partridge whirs up frit away from her nest
And the hare with the morning dew yet on her breast
   Jumps away from his hustle and bustle and noise
   Which he makes in the midst of his rapture and joys,
Now singing and tearing up weeds of all sorts:
Showy corn poppies shining like foxhunters' coats
   And bluecaps and cockleflowers, no matter what,
   To make a gay garland to stick in his hat,
And now he stands out what a gesture he wears
As proud of his colours as soldiers of theirs,
   And why may he not be as vain as the rest:
   Of proud folk we're the proudest, are baubles at best.
Yes summer indeed brings the pleasure to all
That colt feels its freedom now loosed from its stall
   And even this wearisome wayfaring ass
   Can find on the common his bunches of grass,

While round the warped camp neath yon bushes and trees
The Gypsies lie basking themselves at their ease
   And the Gypsy boys shaking their rags to the sun
   Are head over ears in their frolic and fun,
Chasing barefoot along with their dogs by their side
Barking loud as the rabbits bob by them to hide.
   See there sit the swath summer lovers at play
   Neath the shade of those broad-spreading maples all day,
Those brown tawny lasses with lips like a cherry
And fair full as dark as the autumn blackberry,
   The mole hillocks make them soft cushions for love
   And the hedges in arbours hang blooming above,
As blessed as the rich who on sofas reposes,
They toy neath the shades of wild woodbines and roses.
Now look at the sky – it grows muddy with showers,
   And black snails are creeping about in the flowers;
The daisy too look, 'tis a good weather-glass,
It seems even now half asleep in the grass,
   And other flowers too like the sun on the wane
   Are shutting their eyes and seem dreaming again,
While that shepherd boy yonder is startled from sleep
Peeping up at the sky as he bawls to his sheep;
   No doubt he is seeking his hut by the hedge
   All wattled with willows and covered with sedge,
To lie on his bed of cut brakes and be dry,
While the threatened approach of the storm lessens by.
   Now I see you are glad to get sight of the town
   See there's the old spire and below it look down
Our cottage is peeping, aye now you see't plain
As if it was happy to find us again,
   And happy am I we're so nigh to the door
   So run in and take to your play as before
Or rest in your chairs from your toils of the day
By the oak bough that blooms in the chimney so gay.
   See there waning sunbeams, they twitter and fall,
   Through the diamond-paned window to dance on the wall,

The pictures seem smiling its glitter to court
And up jumps the kitten to join in the sport.
   Aye well may you say you are glad we've got home,
   For sweeter it seemeth the farther we roam;
So now we'll sit down and enjoy at our ease
The rest leisure gives us and do as we please.
   Take your toys or read lessons and chatter between
   Of the walk we have had and the things we have seen
And while you are pleasing or resting yourselves
I'll reach down a poet I love from the shelves
   My Thomson or Cowper like flowers in their prime,
   That sat not in closets to study and rhyme,
But roamed out of doors for their verses that yield
A freshness like that which we left in the field;
   That sing both at once to the ear and the eye
   And breathe of the air and the grass and the sky
A music so sweet while we're hid from the rain
That we even seem taking our rambles again.

SPORT IN THE MEADOWS

May-time is in the meadows coming in
   And cowslap peeps have gotten e'er so big
And water blabs and all their golden kin
   Crowd round the shallows by the striding brig;
Daisies and buttercups and lady smocks
   Are all abouten shining here and there
Nodding about their gold and yellow locks
   Like morts of folken crowding at a fair,
The sheep and cows do flocken for a share
   And snatch the blossoms in such eager haste
That basket-bearing children running there
   Do think within their hearts they'll get them all
And hoot and drive them from their graceless waste
   As though there wa'n't a cowslap peep to spare;
For they want some for tea and some for wine
   And some to maken up a cuck-a-ball
To throw across the garland's silken line
   That reaches o'er the street from wall to wall.
Good gracious me how merrily they fare:
   One sees a finer cowslap than the rest
And off they shout, the foremost bidding fair
   To get the prize, and earnest half and jest
The next one pops her down, and from her hand
   Her basket falls and out her cowslaps all
Tumble and litter out; the merry band
   In laughing friendship round about her fall
To helpen gather up the littered flowers
   That she no loss may mourn – and now the crowd
In frolic mood among the merry hours
   Wakens with sudden start and tosses off
Some untied bonnet on its dancing wings;
   Away they follow with a scream and laugh
And aye the youngest ever lags behind
   Till on the deep lake's very brink it hings;

They shout and catch it and then off they start
    The chase for cowslaps merry as before,
And each one seems so anxious at the heart
    As they would even get them all and more.
One climbs a molehill for a bunch of may,
    One stands on tiptoe for a linnet's nest
And pricks her hand and throws her flowers away
    And runs for plantain leaves to have it dressed;
So do they run abouten all the day
    And tease the grass-hid larks from getting rest.
Scarce give they time in their unruly haste
    To tie a shoestring that the grass unties,
And thus they run the meadows' bloom to waste
    Till even comes and dulls their fantasies,
When one finds losses out to stifle smiles
    Of silken bonnet strings – and others sigh
O'er garments renten clambering over stiles,
    Yet in the morning fresh afield they hie
Bidding the last day's troubles a goodbye
    When red-pied cow again them coming hears
And ere they clap the gate she tosses up
    Her head and hastens from the spoil she fears;
The old yoe calls her lamb nor cares to stoop
    To crop a cowslap in their company.
Thus merrily the little noisy troop
    Along the grass as rude marauders hie,
Forever noisy and forever gay
    While keeping in the meadow's holiday.

THE ETERNITY OF NATURE

Leaves from eternity are simple things
To the world's gaze whereto a spirit clings,
   Sublime and lasting – trampled under foot
   The daisy lives and strikes its little root
Into the lap of time – centuries may come
And pass away into the silent tomb
   And still the child hid in the womb of time
   Shall smile and pluck them when this simple rhyme
Shall be forgotten like a churchyard stone
Or lingering lie unnoticed and alone;
   When eighteen hundred years our common date
   Grows many thousands in their marching state,
Aye still the child with pleasure in his eye
Shall cry 'the daisy!' a familiar cry
   And run to pluck it – in the selfsame state
   As when time found it in his infant date
And like a child himself when all was new
Wonder might smile and make him notice too.
   Its little golden bosom frilled with snow
   Might win e'en Eve to stoop adown and show
Her partner Adam in the silky grass
This little gem that smiled where pleasure was;
   And loving Eve from Eden followed ill
   And bloomed with sorrow and lives smiling still,
As once in Eden under heaven's breath,
So now on blighted earth and on the lap of death
   It smiles for ever. Cowslap's golden blooms
   That in the closen and the meadow comes,
Shall come when kings and empires fade and die;
And in the meadows as time's partners lie
   As fresh two thousand years to come as now,
   With those five crimson spots upon its brow
And little brooks that hum a simple lay,
In green unnoticed spots from praise away,

Shall sing – when poets in time's darkness hid
Shall lie like memory in a pyramid,
Forgetting yet not all forgot though lost
Like a thread's end in ravelled windings crossed;
   And the small humble bee shall hum as long
   As nightingales, for time protects the song,
And nature is their soul to whom all clings
Of fair or beautiful in lasting things.
   The little robin in the quiet glen
   Hidden from fame and all the sons of men
Sings unto time a pastoral and gives
A music that lives on and ever lives;
   Both spring and autumn year's rich bloom and fade
   Longer than songs that poets ever made;
And think ye these, time's play-things, pass proud skill?
Time loves them like a child and ever will.
   And so I worship them in bushy spots
   And sing with them when all else notice not,
And feel the music of their mirth agree
With that sooth quiet that bestirreth me;
   And if I touch aright that quiet tone,
   That soothing truth that shadows from their own,
Then many a year shall grow in after days
And still find hearts to love my quiet lays;
   Yet cheering mirth with thoughts sung not for fame
   But for the joy that with their utterance came,
That inward breath of rapture urged not loud
– Birds singing lone fly silent past a cloud
   – So in these pastoral spots which childish time
   Makes dear to me I wander out and rhyme.
What time the dewy morning's infancy
Hangs on each blade of grass and every tree
   And sprents the red thighs of the bumble bee,
   Who 'gins by time's unwearied minstrelsy,
Who breakfasts dines and most divinely sups
With every flower save golden buttercups,

On their proud bosoms he will never go
And passes by with scarcely 'how do ye do';
So in their showy gaudy shining cells
Maybe the summer's honey never dwells
   – Her ways are mysteries all, yet endless youth
   Lives in them all unchangeable as truth.
With the odd number five strange nature's laws
Plays many freaks nor once mistakes the cause
   And in the cowslap peeps this very day
   Five spots appear which time ne'er wears away
Nor once mistakes the counting – look within:
Each peep and five nor more nor less is seen,
   And trailing bindweed with its pinky cup
   Five lines of paler hue goes streaking up,
And birds a-merry keep the rule alive
And lay five eggs nor more nor less than five;
   And flowers, how many own that mystic power
   With five leaves ever making up the flower?
The five-leaved grass trailing its golden cups
Of flowers – five leaves make all for which I stoop;
   And briony in the hedge that now adorns
   The tree to which it clings and now the thorns
Own five star-pointed leaves of dingy white;
Count which I will, all make the number right,
   And spready goosegrass trailing all abroad
   In leaves of silver green about the road,
Five leaves make every blossom all along,
I stoop for many: none are counted wrong.
   'Tis nature's wonder and her maker's will
   Who bade earth be and order owns him still
As that superior power who keeps the key
Of wisdom, power and might through all eternity.

THE EVERGREEN ROSE

Delightful flower 'tis seldom mine
   Such lasting smiles to win,
To see thee through the window shine
   Each morning looking in

And laughing at the window frame
   Right merry at all hours,
No matter whether wind or rain
   Thou'rt never lost to flowers.

Autumn takes summer leaves away
   And strips them like a thief,
But shake thy green locks as he may
   He cannot steal a leaf

As glossy as the ivy's blooms
   That round the oak is seen;
No matter how the weather comes
   Thou'rt still an evergreen.

Birds scarce believe their eyes to meet
   A rose tree still in bloom:
The wren he cocks his tail to see't
   And whistles when he comes;

The robin with his nimble eye
   Looks sidling on the flower,
And sings some bits of melody
   And warms the winter hours.

Then need I dread the winter more
   Or think my dwelling drear,
With evergreens again' the door
   And roses all the year.

THE PRIMROSE BANK

'Tis spring day roams with flowers
   Down every little lane
   And the night is hardly night
But a round of happy hours.

Yes nights are happy nights
   The sky is full of stars
   Like worlds in peace they lie
Enjoying one delight.

The dew is on the thorn
   And the primrose underneath
   Just again' the mossy root
Is shining to the morn

With its little brunny eye
   And its yellow rim so pale
   And its crimp and curdled leaf –
Who can pass its beauties by

Without a look of love?
   When we tread the little path
   That skirts the woodland side
Who can pass, nor look above

To Him who blesses earth
   With these messengers of spring
   And decorates the fields
For our happiness and mirth?

I cannot for I go
   In my fancy once again
   In the woods and little holts
Where the primrose used to grow;

The wood bank seemed so fair
   And the hedgerow in the lane
   Seemed so sweet that scores of times
Have I wished my cottage there,

And felt that lovely mood
   As a birthright God had given
   To muse in the green woods
And meet the smiles of heaven.

And though no culture comes
   To the places where they grow
   Every spring finds more and more
Till the wood all yellow blooms.

The woodman's guessing way
   Oft tramples many down,
   But there's not a blossom missing
When he comes another day.

The woods have happy guests,
   And the birds sing twice as loud
   When they see such crowds of blossoms
Underneath their little nests –

As beauties for the spring –
   Their maker sends them forth
   That man may have his mirth
And nature laugh and sing.

For when roaming where they flower
   They seemed to make woods happy,
   And amid the green light round them
I've spent many a happy hour.

But since I used to stray
   In their hazel haunts for joy,
     The world has found the happy spots
And took the charm away;

It has tracked the pleasant springs
   Like armies on their march,
     Till dearest spots that used to be
Are nought but common things,

Save that their sights employ
   Balm gales and sunny blooms,
     The mind in shaping heavens
As one continued joy.

ON SEEING SOME MOSS IN FLOWER EARLY IN SPRING

Wood walks are pleasant every day
   Where though so full of talk,
Through autumn brown and winter grey
   Meets pleasure in the walk.

O nature's pleasant moods and dreams
   In every journey lies,
Gladding my heart with simple themes
   And cheers and gratifies.

Though poesy's woods and vales and streams
   Grow up within the mind,
Like beauty seen in pleasant dreams
   We nowhere else can find,

Yet common things, no matter what,
   Which nature dignifies,
If happiness be in their lot
   They gratify our eyes.

Some value things for being new
   Yet nature keeps the old,
She watches o'er the humblest too
   In blessings manifold;

The common things of every day,
   However mean or small,
The heedless eye may throw away
   But she esteems them all;

The common things in every place
   Display their sweets abroad:
The daisy shows a happy face
   On every common road,

When winter's past and snows are gone
   It is the first to bring
A merry happy hastener-on,
   The coming of the spring;

And violets – many sorts are known –
   But the sweetest yet that grows
Is that kind which every hedgerow owns
   And everybody knows;

This moss upon the sallow roots
   Of this secluded spot,
Finds seasons that its station suits
   And blossoms unforgot;

This common moss, so hid from view,
   To heedless crowds unknown,
By nature made as happy too
   Finds reasons of its own;

It peeps among the fallen leaves,
   On every stoven grows,
Sufficient sun its shade receives,
   And so it buds and blows.

Thus common things in every place
   Their pleasing lessons give;
They teach my heart life's good to trace
   And learn me how to live;

They feed my heart with one consent:
   That humble hope and fear,
That quiet place and calm content
   Are blessings everywhere.

BALLAD

The spring returns, the pewet screams
  Loud welcome to the dawning,
Though harsh and ill as now it seems
  'Twas music last May morning;
The grass so green, the daisy gay,
  Wakes no joy in my bosom,
Although the garland last May Day
  Wore not a finer blossom.

For by this bridge my Mary sat
  And praised the screaming plover,
As first to hail the May when I
  Confessed myself her lover;
And at that moment stooping down
  I plucked a daisy blossom,
Which smiling she did call her own
  May-garland for her bosom.

And in her breast she hid it there
  As true love's happy omen;
Gold had not claimed a safer care:
  I thought love's name was woman;
I claimed a kiss – she laughed away –
  I sweetly sold the blossom;
I thought myself a king that day:
  My throne was beauty's bosom.

And little thought an evil hour
  Was bringing clouds around me
And least of all that little flower
  Would turn a thorn to wound me;
She showed me after many days –
  Though withered – how she prized it,
And then she leaned to wealthy prize
  And my poor flower despised it.

Aloud the whining pewet screams
    The daisey blossoms as gaily,
But where is Mary? Absence seems
    To ask that question daily;
Nowhere on earth where joy can be
    To glad me with her pleasure,
Another name she owns to me
    She is as stolen treasure.

When love's past the longest mile
    Leaves hope of some returning
Though smiles close by, no hope the while
    Within my heart is burning;
One hour would bring me to her door
    Yet sad and lonely-hearted,
If seas between us both should roar
    We were not further parted.

Though I could reach her with my hand
    Ere suns the earth goes under,
Her heart from mine – the sea and land
    Are not more far asunder;
The wind and clouds now here, now there,
    Hold not such strange dominion
As woman's cold perverted will
    And soon-estranged opinion.

SUMMER BALLAD

Poesy now in summer stoops,
   Full fifty times a day;
The green turns gold with buttercups
   The hedges white with may,
The ballad-singing larks now troop
   By dozens from the hay,
And dozens down as soon as up
   Leaves one the time to play.

But sweeter ballads fill the vale
   When maidens meet the morn,
And the red cow stands o'er the pail
   Beneath the squatty thorn;
When sheep come up and rub their heads
   And cows lie down to chew
Their cuds beneath the battered shade
   When grass is wet with dew.

The magpie's nest is on the top
   She cannot sing, but shows
May's hurry while the maiden stops
   And chatters till she goes;
The May's field ballads, much would need
   If song was all its lot,
And all its bustle rude indeed
   If beauty owned it not.

Morn sprinkles treasures in her way
   Green health in every place,
And I thought verses half the day
   To pass so sweet a face;
Dress sets not off her face so well
   As it sets off her dress,
Love easy knows where beauty dwells
   If fancy bids it guess.

She might have sweethearts, half a score
    And that in half a year,
But she has one and wants no more
    And blushes when he's near;
From idle words she turns away
    And frowns will fools reprove,
But kindness she with kindness pays
    Till almost ta'en for love.

No broaches on her heart she wears,
    Pinned down with golden pins,
She gives herself no foolish airs
    Nor feels the praise she wins;
Though fancy may a flounce prefer
    When May Day comes about,
Pride has but small to do with her
    That's rich enough without.

She loves on Sunday noons to go
    Among the birds in May,
Where buntings 'pink pink pink' as though
    They followed all the way;
She dances round and skips the stile
    Rich in her Sunday dress,
And meets from every face a smile,
    The type of happiness.

And so delightful grows the walk
    With love's familiar ear,
Joy almost may in ballads talk
    When beauty listens near;
And soon as she has past the farm
    And eyes are out of sight,
She takes the waiting shepherd's arm
    And dallies with delight.

She loves to spend an hour or so
   With neighbours and to see
How pinks and cloves and lilies grow
   Which Goody shows so free;
Beds edged with daisies, red and white,
   And thrift and London-pride,
Appears to her so fine a sight
   That nowhere owns beside.

Few are the flowers her taste prefers
   Yet looking up and down
She nips a leaf of lavender
   To put within her gown;
She loves a flower her gown to grace
   But asks not, and receives,
A nosegay sweet, for beauty's face
   In welcome's favour lives.

The young their silent gifts bestow
   That something more would tell,
And old folks happy are to show
   They ever wish it well;
She loves the garden bench at eve
   And takes her sewing there,
And gets by heart the last new song,
   A present from the fair.

She has a love for many things
   But will not own to one,
And he who sees her home at spring
   Is kept a secret on;
She loves the oak upon the green
   In May with apples hung,
For there she sits and sings unseen
   The songs her mother sung.

She loves the thrush that comes to sing
   Upon the hedgerow bough,
And curly-coated lambs of spring
   That race up to the cow;
The shepherd dog in shaggy suit
   In e'er such haste will stand,
And though the old yoe stamps her foot,
   Awaits the patting hand.

The would-be sweetheart often drops
   Love welcomes in her way
And she her ballad only stops
   To pass the time of day;
While some would compliment her health
   And win esteem unseen,
Beauty unconscious of its wealth
   Knows not the maid they mean.

She loves the green that herds the cow
   And gives her labour joy,
Where she plays crookhorn even now
   As wild as any boy;
The sweetest blessings life provides
   Her village peace bestows,
Though some few towns where kin resides
   Is all the world she knows.

And I could go when morning pays
   Green welcome to her song,
And I could stay when evening stays
   Nor think her longest long;
And lie upon the grass and think
   And in the rushes make,
With her sweet looks for pen and ink
   Green ballads for her sake.

IDLE HOUR

Sauntering at ease I often love to lean
   O'er old bridge walls and mark the flood below
Whose ripples through the weeds of oily green
   Like happy travellers mutter as they go,
And mark the sunshine dancing on the arch,
   Time keeping to the merry waves beneath,
And on the bank see drooping blossoms parch,
   Thirsting for water in the day's hot breath,
Right glad of mud drops splashed upon their leaves
   By cattle plunging from the sleepy bank,
While water flowers more than their share receives
   And revel to their very cups in drink;
Just like the world some starve and face but ill
While others riot and have plenty still.

A SPRING MORNING

Spring cometh in with all her hues and smells
In freshness breathing over hills and dells,
   And woods where May her gorgeous drapery hings
   And meads washed fragrant with their laughing springs,
Fresh as new-opened flowers untouched and free
From the bold freedom of the amorous bee;
   The happy time of singing birds is come
   And love's lone pilgrimage now finds a home
Among the mossy oaks, now coos the dove,
And the hoarse crow finds softer notes for love;
   The foxes play around their dens and bark
   In joy's excess amid eve's shadows dark;
The flowers join lips below, the leaves above,
And every sound that meets the ear is love.

ANOTHER SPRING: THE CRAB TREE

Spring comes anew and brings each little pledge
    That still as wont my childish heart deceives;
I stoop again for violets in the hedge
    Among the ivy and old withered leaves,
And often mark amid the clumps of sedge
    The pooty-shells I gathered when a boy;
But cares have claimed me many an evil day
    And chilled the relish which I had for joy,
Yet when crab blossoms blush among the may
    As wont in years gone by, I scramble now,
Up mid the brambles for my old esteems,
    Filling my hands with many a blooming bough,
Till the heart-stirring past as present seems
Save the bright sunshine of those fairy dreams.

SCRAPS OF SUMMER

The southwest wind how pleasant in the face
It breathes while sauntering in a musing place;
   I roam these new-ploughed fields and by the side
   Of this old wood where building birds abide,
And the rich blackbird through his golden bill
Utters wild music when the rest are still;
   Now luscious comes the scent of blossomed beans
   That o'er the path in rich disorder leans
Mid which the bees in busy songs and toils
Load home luxuriantly their yellow spoils;
   The herd cows top the molehills in their play
   And often stand the stranger's steps at bay
Mid clover blossoms red and tawny white
Strong-scented with the summer's warm delight.

The shepherd boys play by the shaded stile
While sunshine gleams with warm and idle smile
   Or hide neath hedges where the linnets sing
   And leaves spread curtains round the bubbling spring,
While winds with idle dalliance waves the woods
And toys with nature in her youthful moods
   Fanning the feathers on the linnet's breast
   And happy maid in lightsome garments dressed
Sweeping her gown in many an amorous shade
As if enamoured of the form displayed;
   Upon the southwest wind the boiling showers
   Brings sweet arrivance of all sorts of flowers
Enjoying like the laughing boys at play
Sabbaths of sunshine's outdoor holiday.

THE POESY OF FLOWERS

What would the rosey be but as the rose?
   A merely sweet undignifying flower.
But clothed by woman's magnifying grace
   It looks upon us with a living power;
Then quickly every blush from beauty glows
   As mirrors – there reflecting beauty's face:
Her lips and luscious cheeks shine in its leaves
   And in the lily – there her bosom heaves.
Flowers thus personify the heart's delight
   And beauty gives us rapture in their sight;
Flowers merely flowers – would seem but cold esteems
   With heart-associations and love-dreams;
But mixed like life with mind – where'er we roam,
They link like household–feelings with our home.

A WOODLAND SEAT

Within this pleasant wood beside the lane
    Let's sit and rest us from the burning sun
And hide us in the leaves and entertain
    An hour away – to watch the wood-brook run
Through heaps of leaves drop dribbling after drop,
    Pining for freedom till it climbs along,
In eddying fury o'er the foamy top,
    And then loud laughing sings its whimpling song,
Kissing the misty dewberry by its side
    With eager salutations and in joy,
Making the flag leaves dance in graceful pride,
    Giving and finding joy – here we employ
An hour right profitable thus to see
Life may meet joys where few intrusions be;

And mark the flowers round us how they live,
    Not only for themselves as we may feel,
But the delight which they to others give,
    For nature never will her gifts conceal
From those who love to seek them – here amid
    These trees how many doth disclose their pride,
From the unthinking rustic only hid,
    Who never turns him from the road aside
To look for beauties which he heedeth not
    – It gives us greater zest to feel the joys
We meet in this sweet solemn suited spot,
    And with high ecstasies one's mind employs
To bear the worst that fickle life prepares,
Finding her sweets as common as her cares.

In every trifle something lives to please
    Or to instruct us – every weed or flower
Heir's beauty as a birthright by degrees,
    Of more or less, though taste alone hath power
To see and value what the herd pass by;
    This common dandelion mark how fine
Its hue – the shadow of the day's proud eye
    Glows not more rich of gold – that nettle there
Trod down by careless rustics every hour
    Search but its slighted blooms – kings cannot wear
Robes pranked with half the splendour of a flower,
    Pencilled with hues of workmanship divine
Bestowed to simple things – denied to flowers
    And sent to gladden hearts so mean as mine.

THE EVENING PRIMROSE

When once the sun sinks in the west
And dewdrops pearl the evening's breast,
  Almost as pale as moonbeams are
  Or its companionable star,
The evening primrose ope's anew
Its delicate blossoms to the dew,
  And shining hermit of the light
  Wastes its fair bloom upon the night,
Who blindfold to its fond caresses
Knows not the beauty it possesses;
  Thus it blooms on till night is by
  And joy looks out with open eye,
'Bashed at the gaze it cannot shun
It faints and withers and is done.

SONNET
FOREST FLOWERS

Ye simple weeds that make the desert gay
   Disclaimed of all e'en by the youngster's eye
Who hefts his stick a weapon in his play
   And lops your blossoms as he saunters by
In mockery of merriment – yet I
   Hail you as favourites of my early days
And every year as mid your haunts I lie
   Some added pleasure claims my lonely gaze:
Star-pointed thistle with its ruddy flowers,
   Wind-waving rush left to bewildered ways
Shunning the scene which culture's toil devours,
   Ye thrive in silence where I glad recline,
Sharing with finer blooms spring's gentle showers,
   That shows ye're prized by better taste than mine.

THE FEAR OF FLOWERS

The nodding oxeye bends before the wind,
The woodbine quakes lest boys their flowers should find
   And prickly dog-rose, spite of its array,
   Can't dare the blossom-seeking hand away;
While thistles wear their heavy skirts of bloom
Proud as the warhorse wears its haughty plume,
   And by the roadside danger's self defies,
   On commons where pinned sheep and oxen lie
In ruddy pomp and ever-thronging mood,
It stands and spreads like danger in a wood,
   And in the village street where meanest weeds
   Can't stand untouched to fill their husks with seed,
The haughty thistle o'er all danger towers
In every place the very wasp of flowers.

FIRST SIGHT OF SPRING

The hazel blooms in threads of common hue
   Peep through the swelling buds and look for spring,
Ere yet a whitethorn leaf appears in view
   Or March finds throstles pleased enough to sing;
   On the old touchwood tree woodpeckers cling
A moment and their harsh-toned notes renew;
   In happier mood the stock dove claps his wing,
The squirrel sputters up the powdered oak
   With tail cocked over his head and ears erect
Startled to hear the woodman's understroke,
   And with the courage that his fears collect
He hisses fierce, half malice and half glee,
Leaping from branch to branch about the tree,
   In winter's foliage moss and lichens dressed.

PLEASANT SPOTS

There is a wild and beautiful neglect
    About the fields that so delights and cheers
Where nature her own feelings to effect
    Is left at her own silent work for years;
The simplest thing thrown in our way delights
    From the wild careless feature that it wears,
The very road that wanders out of sight
    Crooked and free is pleasant to behold;
And such the very weeds left free to flower
    Corn poppies red and carlock gleaming gold
That makes the cornfield shine in summer's hour
    Like painted skies – and fancy's distant eye
    May well imagine armies marching by
In all the grand array of pomp and power.

THE CLUMP OF FERN

Pleasures lie scattered all about our way,
   Harvest for thought and joy to look and glean,
Much of the beautiful to win our praise
   Lie where we never headed aught had been;
By this wood stile half-buried in the shade
   Of rude disorder – bramble, woodbine, all
So thickly wove that nutters scarcely made
   An entrance through – and now the acorns fall,
The gatherers, seeking entrance, pause awhile,
Ere they mount up the bank to climb the stile,
   Half-wishing that a better road was nigh,
Yet here mid leaf-strewn morning's autumn mild,
   While pleasing sounds and pleasing sights are by,
Things beautiful delight my heart to smile.

Here underneath the stile's moss-covered post
   A little bunch of fern doth thrive in spring,
Hid from the noisy wind and coming frost
   Like late-reared young neath the wood pigeon's wing;
   I've seen beneath the furze bush clumps of ling
So beautiful in pinky knots of bloom,
   That made the inmost heart's emotions breathe
   A favourite love for the unsocial heath,
That gives man no inviting hopes to come
   To fit his dwelling and disturb the scene;
   So in my loneliness of mood this green
Large clump of crimpled fern leaves doth bequeath
   Like feelings – and wherever wanderers roam
Some little scraps of happiness is seen.

THE YARROW

Dweller in pastoral spots, life gladly learns
   That nature never mars her aim to please;
Thy dark leaves like to clumps of little ferns
   Imbues my walks with feelings such as these;
O'ertopped with swarms of flowers that charms the night,
Some blushing into pink and others white,
   On meadow banks, roadsides and on the leas
Of rough neglected pastures – I delight
   More even than in gardens thus to stray
Amid such scenes and mark thy hardy blooms,
   Peering into the autumn's mellowing day;
The mower's scythe swept summer blooms away
   Where thou, defying dreariness, wilt come
Bidding the loneliest russet paths be gay.

THE RAGWORT

Ragwort thou humble flower with tattered leaves,
   I love to see thee come and litter gold;
What time the summer binds her russet sheaves
   Decking rude spots in beauties manifold,
   That without thee were dreary to behold,
Sunburnt and bare – the meadow bank, the baulk
   That leads a waggonway through mellow fields
   Rich with the tints that harvest's plenty yields
Browns of all hues – and everywhere I walk
   Thy waste of shining blossoms richly shields
The suntanned sward in splendid hues that burn
   So bright and glaring that the very light
Of the rich sunshine doth to paleness turn
   And seems but very shadows in thy sight.

THE BRAMBLE

Spontaneous flourisher in thickets lone
   Curving a most impenetrable way
To all save nutters when a tree has shown
   Ripe clusters to the autumn's mellow day;
   And long the brustle of the rude affray
Clings to the branches – scraps of garments torn
   Of many hues: red, purple, green and grey,
From scrambling maid who ties the branches down
   And inly smiles at the strange garb she wears,
While rough in hasty speech the brushing clown
   Leg hoppled as in tethers turns and swears
And cuts the bramble strings with oath and frown,
   Yet scorn wronged bush, taste marks thee worthy praise,
   Green mid the underwood of winter days.

HEAVY DEW

The night hath hung the morning smiles in showers,
　The kingcups burnished all so rich within
Hang down their slender branches on the grass,
　The bumble bees on the huge thistle flowers,
Clings as half-sleeping yet and motion lacks,
　Not even stirring as I closely pass,
Save that they lift their legs above their backs
　In trembling dread when touched – yet still they lie
Fearful of danger without power to fly;
　The shepherd makes a mort of crooked tracks,
His dog half-drowned and dripping to the skin
　Stops oft and shakes his shaggy hide in vain,
Wading through grass like rivers to the chin
　Then snorts and barks and brushes on again.

THE HEDGE WOODBINE

The common woodbine in the hedgerow showers
   A multitude of blossoms and from thence
   The tinctured air all fragrance on the sense
Flings richest sweets that almost overpowers,
   And faintness palls the taste which goes away
When some old ballad beautifully sung
Comes through the hedge with crowded fragrance hung,
   From merry maidens tossing up the hay;
To list the sunny mirth we inly feel
   That none but beauty's self could sing so well,
   And pastoral visions on our fancies dwell;
Our joys, excess joys, inmost thoughts conceal;
   The woodbine hedge – the maids half toil, half play,
   Woods like to clouds obscure and wear away.

THE WATER LILIES ON THE MEADOW STREAM

The water lilies on the meadow stream
   Again spread out their leaves of glossy green,
And some yet young in a rich copper gleam
   Scarce open in the sunny stream is seen,
Throwing a richness upon leisure's eye
   That thither wanders in a vacant joy;
While on the sloping banks luxuriant lie
   Tending of horse or cow the chubby boy,
Who in delighted whims will often throw
   Pebbles to hit and splash their sunny leaves,
Yet quickly dry again they shine and glow
   Like some rich vision that his eye deceives,
Spreading above the water day by day,
Safer than blooms among the meadow hay.

SPRING

The sweet spring now is coming
   In beautiful sunshine;
Thorns bud and wild flowers blooming,
   Daisy and celadine;
Something so sweet there is about the spring,
Silence is music ere the birds will sing.

And there's the hedgerow pooties,
   Blackbirds from mossy cells,
Pink there where the last year's shoot is,
   Hedge bottoms and wood dells;
Striped, spotted, yellow, red, to spring so true,
For which the schoolboy looks with pleasures new.

On gates the yellowhammer
   As bright as celadine
Sits – green linnets learn to stammer
   And robins sing divine;
On brown land furrows stalks the crow
And magpies on the moor below.

In small hedged closes lambkins stand,
   The cud the heifer chews,
Like snow clumps upon fallow land
   They shine among the ewes,
Or sheets of water by moonlight
The lambkins shine so very white.

The lane, the narrow lane
   With daisy beds beneath,
You scarce can see the light again
   Until you reach the heath;
Thorn hedges grow and meet above
For half a mile a green alcove.

The nettles by garden walls
    Stand angrily and dun,
Summer on them like prison falls
    And all their blossoms shun;
The Abbey's haunted heaps of stone
Is by their treachery overgrown.

There's verdure in the stony street
    Deceiving earnest eyes:
The bare rock has its blossoms sweet
    The microscope espies;
Flowers, leaves and foliage everywhere
That clothes the animated year.

Fields, meadows, woods and pastures,
    There's spring in every place,
From winter's wild disasters
    All bear her happy face;
Beasts on their feet and birds upon the wing,
The very clouds upon the sky look spring.

Sunshine prefers by the hedge
    And there the pilewort's sure to come,
The primrose by the rustling sedge
    And largest cowslips first in bloom:
All show that spring is everywhere,
The flowery herald of the year.

VALENTINE

A dewdrop on a rose leaf
   The one will dry – the other fade,
And time is like that silent thief
   To rob the rosy blooming maid;
But such plain truth I must decline
A sermon's not a Valentine.

I would say something very fine
   But cannot fancy what to send;
I've chose thee long my valentine
   And this comes from a silent friend;
Primroses and hepaticas –
I've gathered thee in earlier days.

Cupids, quivers, painted darts
   Are ornaments for idle fancies;
Flaming altars, bleeding hearts
   Are not of love – but its romances;
Yet spring's first flowers will well agree
With valentines I send to thee.

The snowdrops like to frozen dew,
   The crocus like as blazing stars,
The daisies all the season through
   Are valentines so very rare;
Some grow in gardens, some by brooks
And richly paint thy happy looks.

The field flowers, they are heaven's smiles,
   Like sunbeams in the field of spring,
Unused to sorrow, or to toils,
   Their minstrels are the birds who sing
With all their charms, spring's dress divine:
I send thee love a Valentine.

TO E. L. E. ON MAY MORNING

"Sit under the May bush at the head of the table"
                                    Darley

1
Lady 'tis thy desire to move
  Far from the world's ungentle throng,
Lady 'tis thy delight to love
  The muses and the heirs of song;
Nor taste alone is thine to praise
  For thou canst touch the minstrel wire,
And while thou'rt praising others' lays
  Wakes notes that any may admire;
Forgive if I in friendship's way
Do offer thee a wreath of May.

2
I greet thee with no gaudy flowers
  For thou art not to fashions prone,
But rather lovest the woodland bowers
  Where nature's beauties charm alone;
The passion flower and ceres fine
  By wealth and pride are reared alone,
Yet flowers more sweet nor less divine,
  Spring's humble fields and forests own,
To every hand and bosom given
And nourished by the dews of heaven.

3
The little violet too I weave
  In wreaths I'm fain that thou shouldst prize,
Although it comes at winter's eve
  And often in the tempest dies;
The primrose too a doubtful dream
  Of what precarious spring would be,

Yet would I not these types should seem
   Aught fancy feigns resembling thee,
And thus belie thy gentle heart
Where coldness seems to have no part.

4

Here too are boughs of blushing may
   And lilies of the valley fair,
Yet not with idle praise to say
   They're types of what are sweet and fair;
I cropped one from the pasture hedge
   The others from the forest dell,
And thou hast given the muses pledge
   Such scenes delight thy bosom well;
'Tis not thy person wakes my lays
Thy heart alone I mean to praise.

5

Forgive me though I flatter not,
   Youth's beauties ladies least can spare,
Hath been by riper years forgot
   Though thou hast had a happy place;
And I might praise full-many a grace
   That lives and lingers yet behind,
But they like flowers shall change their place,
   Not so the beauties of the mind;
So I have ivy placed between
To prove that worth is evergreen.

6

The little blue forget-me-not
   Comes too on friendship's gentle plea,
Spring's messenger in every spot
   Smiling on, all remember me;
But gaudy tulips find no place
   In garlands friendship would bestow,

Yet here the cowslip shows its face
   Prized for its sweetness more than show;
Passions to pride and pomp inclined
Too often prove the want of mind.

7

I would not on May's garland fling
   The laurel to the muses and thee
For fashion's praise – a common thing –
   Hath made of that once sacred tree;
And trust me many laurels wear
   That never grew on Parnass' hill,
Yet dare and speed 'tis thine to wear
   The muses' laurels if ye will;
Let flattery think her wreaths divine:
Merit by its own worth will shine.

8

O when I read the glorious host
   Of poets to my country born,
Though sorrow was the lot of most,
   And many shared the sneers of scorn,
That now by time and talent tried
   Give life to fame's eternal sun;
O when I mark the glorious pride
   That England from her bards hath won,
E'en the meanest of the throng
Warm into ecstasy and song.

9

The highest gifts each kingdom claims
   Are minstrels on the muses' throne,
And bards who've won the richest fames
   'Tis England's richest pride to own
Shakespeares and Miltons, they that heir
   The fames immortal o'er decay,

And Scotts and Byrons born to bear
　The honours of a later day,
That joins to present past renown
　And sings eternity to crown.

10
These from proud laurels never won
　Their fames and honours more divine,
They like the grand eternal sun
　Confer their glories where they shine;
The laurel were a common bough
　Had it not decked the poets' crown
And even weeds so common now
　Placed there would augur like renown;
Bloom satellites in glory's way
Proud as the laurel and the bay.

11
Lady and thou hast chosen well
　To give the muses thy regard;
There taste from pleasure bears the bell,
　There feeling finds its own reward;
Though genius often while it makes
　Life's millions happy with her songs,
From sorrow's cup her portion takes
　And struggles under bitterest wrongs;
To cares of life and song – unknown –
The poet's fame be thine alone.

THE NOSEGAY OF WILD FLOWERS

In schoolboy days as on a mother's breast,
   When nature nursed me in her flowery pride,
I culled her bounty such as seemed best
   And made my garlands by some hedgerow side;
With pleasing eagerness the mind reclaims
   From black oblivion's shroud such artless scenes,
And cons the calendar of childish names
   With simple joy when manhood intervenes.

From the sweet time that spring's young joys are born
   And golden catkins deck the sallow tree,
Till summer's blue-caps blossom mid the corn
   And autumn's ragwort yellows o'er the lea,
I roamed the fields about, a happy child,
   And bound my posies up wi' rushy ties
And laughed and muttered o'er my visions wild,
   Bred in the brain of pleasure's ecstasies.

Crimp-frilled daisy, bright bronze buttercup,
   Frecked cowslap peeps gilt, wins of morning's dew
And hooded aron early sprouting up,
   Ere the whitethorn bud half unfolds to view,
Wi' eager joy each filled my playful hand,
   And wan-hued lady smocks that love to spring
'Side the swamp margin of some plashy pond
   With all the blooms that early Aprils bring.

The jaundiced-tinctured primrose sickly sere,
   Mid its broad curdled leaves of mellow green,
Hemmed in wi' relics of the parted year,
   The mournful wrecks of summers that has been;

Dead leaves of ash and oak and hazel tree
    The constant covering of all woody land,
With tiny violets creeping plenteously
    That one by one enticed my patient hand.

As shadowy April's suns and showers did pass
    And summer's wild profusions plenteous grew
Hiding the spring flowers in weeds and grass,
    What meads and copses would I wander through,
When on the waters op'd the lily buds
    And fine long purples shadowed in the lake,
When freckled cuckoos peeped in the woods
    Neath darkest shades that boughs and leaves could make.

Then did I wear day's many hours away
    In gathering blooms of seemly sweetest kinds,
In ambling for blossoms of the whitethorn may
    Ere they fell victims to unfeeling winds;
And twisting woodbines and the flushed briar rose
    How sweet remembrance on the mind doth rise,
As they bowed arching where the runnel flows;
    To think how oft I waded for the prize.

The ragged robins by the spinney lake,
    And flag flower bunches deeper down the flood
And snugly hiding in the feathered brake
    Full-many a bluebell found and cuckoo-bud,
And old man's beard that wreathed along the hedge,
    Their oddly rude misshapen tawny flowers
And prickly burs that crowd the leaves of sedge,
    That claimed my pleasing search for hours and hours.

And down the hayfields wading above the knees
    Through seas of waving grass - what days I've gone!
Cheating the hopes of many labouring bees
    By cropping blossoms they were perched upon,

As thyme upon the hills and lambtoe knots
And the wild stalking canterbury-bell
By hedgerow side and bushy bordering spots,
That loves in shade and solitude to dwell.

'Tis sweet to view as in a favoured book
 Life's rude beginning page long turned o'er;
'Tis nature's common feeling back to look
 On things that pleased us when they are no more,
Pausing on childish scenes a wished repeat,
 Seeming more sweet to value when we're men
As one awakened from a vision sweet
 Wisheth to sleep and dream it o'er again.

And when the summer's swarms half-nameless fled
 And autumn's landscape faded bleak and wild
And leaves 'gin fall and show their berries red,
 Still wi' the season would I be beguiled
To seek lone spots, home leaving far behind
 Where wildness rears her brakes and teazle burs
And where last lingering of the flowery kind
 Blue heath bells tremble neath the sheltering furze.

Sweet was such walks on the half-barren wild
 Which ploughs leave quiet with their briars and brakes;
Prospects of freedom, pleasing from a child,
 To track the crook'd path which the rabbit makes;
On such times past, one loves to look behind,
 Nor lives a soul mere trifles as they be,
But feels a joy in bringing to his mind
 The wild flower rambles of his infancy.

FIELD THOUGHTS

Field thoughts to me are happiness and joy
   Where I can lie upon the pleasant grass,
Or track some little path and so employ
   My mind in trifles pausing as I pass;
The little wild flower clumps by nothing nursed
   But dews and sunshine and impartial rain,
And welcomly to quench my summer thirst
   I bend me by the flaggy dyke to gain
Dewberries so delicious to the taste,
   And then I wind the flag-fringed meadow lake
And mark the pike plunge with unusual haste
   Through water weeds and many a circle make,
While bursts of happiness from heaven fall:
There all have hopes, here fields are free for all.

OPEN WINTER

Where slanting banks are always with the sun
　　The daisy is in blossom even now,
And where warm patches by the hedges run,
　　The cottager when coming home from plough,
Brings home a cowslap root in flower to set;
Thus ere the Christmas goes the spring is met,
　　Setting up little tents about the fields
In sheltered spots. Primroses when they get
　　Behind the wood's old roots where ivy shields
Their crimpled, curdled leaves, will shine and hide;
　　Cart-ruts and horse-footings scarcely yield
A slur for boys just crizzled and that's all;
　　Frost shoots his needles by the small dyke side
And snow in scarce a feather's seen to fall.

THE LITTLE PATHS ARE PRINTED EVERY ONE

The little paths are printed every one
  Right full of passing feet and patten rings,
As happiness to crushing fairs had gone;
  Although the mavis on the ash tree sings
Of hidden storms unlooked for coming on,
  Now to the snug green close and greener still
The level meadow merry bosoms hie,
  Where by the hedge, odd bush or old mole hill
The cowslaps seem the finest to the eye;
There do they run and whoop and almost fly,
  The finest and the finest still to pull,
And wake the meadow echoes with old tunes,
As merry as the cuckoos are in June,
  Then take away with hands and baskets full.

WHEN MILKING COMES THEN HOME THE MAIDEN WENDS

When milking comes then home the maiden wends
With kerchief stuffed with fairings for her friends,
   And while her umbrella shuns the showers
   Pulls off her glove to gather meadow flowers;
She shakes them from the rain and bears them on
For many a passing clown to smile upon,
   Who waits the fair folks in their idle hours
   And begs her fairings and admires her flowers,
And begs that she would help them in their toil
And makes excuse to snatch them for a smile;
   But soon the favoured swain appears in view
   And meets the ready fairing as his due,
And when the cows are done the hours to spare,
To spend in telling news about the fair.

THE DREARY FEN A WASTE OF WATER GOES

The dreary fen a waste of water goes
With nothing to be seen but royston crow;
   The traveller journeying on the road for hours
   Sees nothing but the dykes and water flowers;
The lonely lodges scattered miles away
Look up from fear and robbers all the day;
   The merry maiden that no place dislikes
   Runs out and fills her kettle from the dykes;
She hurries wildly from the face of men
And knows no company but cocks and hens;
   Here highland maidens see in Sunday's hours
   The glorious sight of sinkfoin grounds in flower,
And meets the savoury smells that wake the morn,
The woodbine hedges and the poppied corn.

A WALK

Being refreshed with thoughts of wandering moods
I took my staff and wandered far away
Through swampy fen land void of heaths and woods,
To see if summer's luxury could display
In such drear places aught of beautiful;
And sooth it gives me much delight to say
That painters would feel exquisite to cull
Rich bits of landscape I have seen today:
Down by the meadow-side our journey lay,
Along a sloping bank profusely spread
With yarrow, ragwort, fleabane, all in flower,
As showy almost as a garden bed,
But thistles like unbidden guests would come
And throw a dreary prospect in the way;

Then o'er some arches' intersecting walls
We clambered and pursued the dreary fen,
Upon whose dreary edge old Waldron hall
Stood like a lone place far removed from men,
Hid under willows tall as forest trees,
Yet there we met with places rich to please:
Green closen osier clumps and black-topped reeds
In little forests shooting, crowds on crowds,
So thickly-set, no opening scarce allowed
The bird a passage in their shade to breed;
And now a fisher's hut – I could but look –
In lone seclusion in my journey lay,
Placed on a knoll of that wild reedy nook,
As if some Crusoe had been cast away.

In that rude desolate flat when winter floods
Rave seas of danger round its little bay,
So thought I in surprise's startled moods
To meet that little picture in my way;

Then swept the brown bank in a winding way
And flag clumps, vivid green and little woods
Of osiers made the wilderness be gay,
And some green closen, so intensely green,
I could have wasted half a summer's day
To gaze upon their beauty so serene,
As if calm peace had made its dwelling there,
For in such places she hath often been
An unbound dweller in the open air,
A hermit giving blessings to the scene.

Now came the river sweeping round the nooks
By thirsty summer's pilgrimage subdued,
Dark and yet clear the glassy water looks
As slow and easy in majestic mood,
It sweeps along by osier-crowded glen,
Until it winds an almost naked flood
Along the flats of the unwooded fen;
Yet even there prolific summer dwells
And garnishes its sides in vivid green
Of flags and reeds, the otter's pathless den,
– Now lanes without a guidepost plainly tells
Their homeward paths – while from a stile is seen
The open church tower and its little bells,
And chimneys low where peaceful quiet dwells.

My journey feels refreshed with green delight,
Though woods nor heaths nor molehill pastures led
A pleasant varied way – yet richly spread
Corn-crowded grounds in 'awthorn hedges dight,
That shelter gave to many a little bird
Where yellow hammers 'peeped' in saddened plight
At peeping cowboy that its pleasure marred,
Who carried in his hat his stubbly nest

And sung in rapture o'er his stolen prize
The eggs in his rude mind where strangely guest
As written on by some strange fantasies,
Strange prodigies that happy summer brings,
To minds as happy and my journey tells
My mind that joy in poor seclusion dwells.

THE DAISY

The daisy is a happy flower
   And comes at early spring
And brings with it the sunny hour
   When bees are on the wing.

It brings with it the butterfly
   And humble early bee
With the polyanthus' golden eye
   And blooming apple tree.

Hedge sparrows form the mossy nest
   In the old garden hedge,
Where schoolboys in their idle glee
   Seek pooties as their pledge.

The cow stands blooming all the day
   Over the orchard gate,
And eats her bits of sweet mown hay
   And Goody stands to wait

Lest what's not eaten the rude wind
   May rise and snatch away,
Over the neighbour's hedge behind
   Where hungry cattle lay.

EDITORIAL NOTE

Clare's poetry is difficult to punctuate. His sentences in verse spill over the normal grammatical pauses for breath one might expect in a poem (such as in the sonnet 'Idle Hour'). Though often the pauses are indicated by the natural rhythms of the line and by clausal structures, it is often very tricky indeed to insert the forced pause of a colon, dash or full-stop. Where it is too problematic, I have avoided forcing pauses, as Clare's syntax deliberately flows over the normal boundaries of punctuation. Having said this, Clare's syntax is remarkable for its clarity even when completely unpunctuated. In this edition the indentation of type to highlight rhyme assists us in seeing just how close to the chosen form Clare's rhythmic line adheres. 'Childhood' (p. 23) is typical, in that each major syntactical pause, or each beginning of a new clause, will come between the end of the fourth and the beginning of the fifth line. Almost every stanza is therefore neatly divided into two blocks of alternating rhyme (*ababcdcd*), and each of these blocks is often a syntactical or clausal unit unto itself. By and large all a punctuating editor has to do with such poems, is to insert a semi-colon at the end of the fourth line of each stanza and a full-stop at the end of each stanza, which is what I have done. Clare's comfort with and mastery of his chosen forms is clear in a poem like 'Childhood'. The chosen forms – stanza, line length, rhythm, rhyme, register – become the grammatical punctuation. So this edition is punctuated, yet fairly lightly.

Standardising Clare's spelling is a also complicated job. Although I have employed a fairly rigorous editorial policy of standardising consistently, it is important that a reader be aware of what effects might be lost as a result. Again the poem 'Childhood' provides one such instance among many. In this edition, the poem begins: 'The past it is a magic word / Too beautiful to last'. Clare points us not only to the past, but to its existence as a *word*. And what he says is that the word itself will not last through history. In my editing of that very line I have actually made sure Clare is right. In Clare's manuscript the word 'magic' is spelled 'majic'. In this edition you will find I have 'corrected' (in other words enforced current orthographic standards found in dictionaries) the word to 'magic'. But what is lost? Perhaps we lose the sense of a deliberately conceived distance when we standardise such a spelling; perhaps Clare intended just such a distancing effect of antiquity and mystery that is conveyed immediately we see 'majic', but not when we read 'magic'; 'magic' just does not carry the same effect, the same aura of a magical, distant past. The word spelled 'majic' is simply *more* magic than when it is spelled 'magic'. Seamus Heaney implies that a similar effect is wrought when Clare spells butterfly 'butter flye'; Heaney writes '[r]arely has the butteriness of a butterfly been so available' (*John Clare in Context,* p. 137). Spelling can highlight a poetic effect so delicately, in the most intricate fashion, that any standardisation is sure to change the overall impact of the poem. In the line from 'Childhood' the original manuscript spelling enacts a defamiliarising effect which is exactly what the poem seems to conclude with – that distance between the vision of the child and the dull eye of the careworn adult. In a typically Clarean phrase, the speaker of 'Childhood' concludes 'I grow a stranger to myself'. So the distance between the reader and the text, which assists in conveying the distance between the older speaker and his younger self, is lessened when we standardise. Strangely enough, although discussing a different poem and a different word ('proged' in 'The Mouse's Nest'), Heaney suggests that if Clare had standardised himself 'both he and his readers would have been distanced in a minimal yet crucial way from the here and nowness, or there and thenness, of what happened' (Ibid., p. 133). It is perhaps just as true that we cannot know for sure when Clare's spelling was deliberately non-standard, or when the divergences and idiosyncrasies were accidental or deliberate. Editors in the past forty years have effectively seen Clare's often erratic and inconsistent spelling as a political and class-based stance against the culturally-empowered classes' standardising of the language in the eighteenth century. Simply put, editors have based their transcriptions of exactly what Clare wrote in manuscript on the fact that the writer was a farm labourer; his spelling was his own, it was of his people. Furthermore, editors have suggested that if we standardise his language now, we do him and his class a disservice. But there is little evidence in Clare's own words to support such a politicisation of his spelling practice. What is much more likely is that Clare would have been horrified to see his works produced without the orthographic and typographic polish that his first and most successful editor John Taylor gave his work. At the same time – and here's the rub – Clare's verse is rich *because* he uses words and pronunciations of his locality, of his particular rural and village life, and of everyday Helpston working-class speech. These words enrich his verse *because* they are not standard. Some readers and editors think the same of his non-standard spelling, so they retain it. The editorial debate looks set to continue as long as Clare's works are edited, and so it should. If you are interested in Clare today, you really ought to be reading his poems in several different versions, to find the editorial style (or style of reconstruction) that suits you most. A reader might even consult the publicly-available manuscripts or microfilm copies; only then would s/he discover just how far from the original hand-written manuscript any published text inherently is, and what creative and reconstructive power lies in the role of the editor. Perhaps it is futile to try to reconstruct Clare's posthumous wishes; instead maybe editors should focus upon the needs of Clare's current audience.

GLOSSARY AND NOTES

For this brief glossary I have heavily relied on the following three sources, and after each entry (other than those where a general reference work sufficed) I have indicated the source of information. I have often quoted Anne Elizabeth Baker in full, as she corresponded with Clare while he was resident at Northampton General Lunatic Asylum (1841-1864) for the research towards her *Glossary,* and so probably comes closer to Clare's intended meanings than any linguist or glossary-maker since 1854. For the use of the glossary in Geoffrey Summerfield's edition of Clare, recently republished as a Penguin Classic, I am grateful for the permission of Professor Judith Summerfield. Richard Mabey's magnificent work was invaluable.

AEB Anne Elizabeth Baker, *Glossary of Northamptonshire Words and Phrases* (2 vols., London: John Russell Smith; Northampton: Abel & Sons, and Mark Dorman, 1854).

GS Geoffrey Summerfield, ed., *John Clare: Selected Poems* (London: Penguin Books, 1990).

RM Richard Mabey, *Flora Britannica* (London: Sinclair-Stevenson, 1996).

'**aw,** haw, fruit of the hawthorn
bee-spell, 'the pattern in a glass marble, which resembled a swarm of bees, more clearly seen when it was wetted by licking' [GS].
bittersweet, 'woody nightshade, *Solanum dulcamara*... has rather tempting scarlet berries, like miniature plum tomatoes... flowers are purple, with the petals reflexed behind a yellow cone' [RM]
blue-caps, 'corn blue-bottle. *Centurea Cyanus*' [AEB]
blue heath bells, probably the harebell, *Campanula Rotundifola* (see front cover photo by Peter Moyse). In 'Nosegay of Wild Flowers' (p. 91) it is said to be the 'last lingering of the flowery kind' which concurs with Mabey: the latter writes that the 'sky-blue bells shaking slightly on their stalks are, fittingly, one of the last flowers of the year, blooming on into the first autumn gales'.
Bonneparte, colloquial (or childlike) pronunciation of Bonaparte, Napoleon, First Emperor of France, 1769–1821
briony, variant spelling of bryony, any climbing plant of genus *Bryonia*
brustle, 'to rustle; bustle' [GS]
bumbarrel, Long Tailed Tit
canterbury-bell, '*Campanula medium*... naturalised in waste ground and grassy places... flowers are deep and lipped, like small teacups, and may have been named after the similarly-shaped horse-bells of pilgrims to St Thomas à Becket's shrine' [RM]
carlock, variant spelling of 'charlock' (see below)
cat gallow sticks, 'two sticks stuck vertically in the ground and a third placed horizontally upon them. It is a favourite boyish pastime to jump over them' [AEB].
charlock, wild mustard, *Sinapsis arvensis,* 'a common native annual of arable fields and waysides. The rough and bitter leaves have been used as a green vegetable in times of food shortages' [RM]
chitter, 'to chirp' [GS]
clock-a-clay, 'a childish name for the lady-bird' [AEB]

closen, 'small enclosed fields (an old plural ending)' [GS]
cockleflowers, 'corncockle, *Agrostemma githago* (... Kiss-me-quick). One of the most attractive of cornfield annuals, with purple flowers which are folded or furled like a flag before they open... these days it is seen only occasionally' [RM]
crabs, crab apples
crizzle, 'To crisp. Water that is slightly frozen is just crizzled over; parsley that is fried is nicely crizzled' [AEB]
Crusoe, protagonist of *The Life and strange and surprising Adventures of Robinson Crusoe,* desert island castaway novel by Daniel Defoe, 1719
cuck-a-ball, 'May-game ball, made of flowers' [GS]
cuckoo-bud, buttercup, or 'crow-foot. The several species of Ranunculi grown in meadows' [AEB]
cuts, woodcuts, illustrations
Darley, George Darley, Irish-born poet and dramatist, part of the *London Magazine* circle, 1795-1846
De Wint, De Wint, Peter, English landscape painter, 1784–1849
ducks and drakes, 'A youthful amusement of casting flat stones or slates upon the surface of a piece of still water, that they may skim along, making circles as they dip and emerge without sinking: the first time the stone rebounds from the water, the boy cries out '*a duck*'; the second time, '*a duck and a drake*'; the third, 'a halfpenny cake'; and the fourth, 'and a penny to pay the baker'. This appears to be a pastime of great antiquity...' [AEB]
eldern, of the elder tree, *sambucus,* has white flowers and red or blue-black berries
E.L.E., Eliza Louisa Emmerson, Clare's most communicative London-based friend and patron
fairing, present bought at a fair
Fenning's Spelling Book, possibly an edition of Daniel Fenning's *A New Grammar of the English language; or, an easy introduction to the art of speaking and writing English with propriety and correctness* (London, 1771) of which there were many editions

firetail, the Redstart [AEB] (bird)

flag, flaggy, 'Applied to corn that grows luxuriantly, that the blade is large and thick, like *flags* or rushes' [AEB]

fleabane, '*Pulcaria dysenterica*, is a frequent perennial of ditches, damp hedge-banks and meadows, with wrinkled, downy-green leaves and neat marigold flowers' [RM]

frecked, freckled (orig. in MS 'freckt')

furze flowers, yellow flowers of gorse. '"When gorse is in blossom, kissing's in season" is a saying known throughout Britain... one of the great signature plants of commonland and rough open space, places where lovers can meet, walk freely and lose themselves, if need be, in its dense thickets' [RM]

hepatica, any plant of a genus (*Hepatica*) of herbs of the buttercup family

hing, 'to hang. Current in Scotland... Clare furnishes various examples of its present use; probably variations for the sake of rhyme' [AEB]

hopple, 'to tie the legs together' [AEB]

kingcup, 'marsh marigold. *Caltha palustris*. The same name is sometimes given to the butter-cup' [AEB}

lady-cow, ladybird [AEB]

lady smocks, AEB has this as the common bindweed, but in 'The Nosegay of Wild Flowers' (p. 91) that Clare is referring to 'wan-hued' flowers 'that love to spring' beside 'the swamp margin of some plashy pond'; they are therefore more likely to be *Cardamine pratensis* (otherwise known as cuckooflowers), which according to Mabey grow in 'damp grassland, roadsides, ditches and river-banks... flowers vary in colour from very pale pink to mauve, and are slightly cupped or "frocked" (though 'smock' was once less than complimentary slang for a woman, on a par with our "a bit of skirt", and there may be allusions in the name to what went on in springtime meadows)' [RM]. For confirmation, see 'Sport in the Meadows', p. 48 of this edition.

lambtoe, 'Probably another name for the *Lotus corniculatus*. Clare is my only authority for this word' [AEB]. Also known as 'Common bird's-foot-trefoil', among 60 other names [RM].

London-pride, 'or London tuft. Sweet William. *Saxifraga umbrosa.* 'None-so-pretty' bears the same name, in other places, particularly in London' [AEB]

long legged shepherd, crane-fly, daddy-long-legs, harvestman, of *Tipulidae* family

may, the hawthorn or its blossom

mort, 'a quantity, a great number... A low, colloquial word. Clare frequently adopts it' [AEB]

Nash, John Nash, English architect and city planner, 1752–1835

nauntle, 'To elevate, to hold yourself erect. Clare, who is my only authority for this word, makes frequent use of it, both verbally and adjectivally' [AEB]

oxeye, '*Leucanthemum vulgare*, (...Dog daisy, Horse daisy, Moon daisy, Moonpenny, Marguerite)... bright, brisk flower that can seem to glow in the fields on midsummer evenings. It is one of the first meadow flowers to colonise unsprayed grassland' [RM]

Parnass', Parnassus, mountain in Greece, sacred to the Muses

parsons and clerks, possibly a children's game?

pewet, variant spelling of puwit or pute, all 'imitative designation for the lapwing or plover. *Tringa vanellus*' (bird) [AEB]

pooty, snail or snail shell: 'girdled snail shell, *Helix nemoralis*... I give it on the authority of Clare, who furnishes various illustrations' [AEB]

pranked, 'dressed out, adorned' [AEB]

ragwort, *Senecio jacobea,* malodorous and poisonous common yellow flower of paddocks and pastures, 'regarded as the great enemy by those who keep horses' [RM]

royston crow, 'The Hooded Crow. Cornix corvus. (Linn.) A bird of rare occurrence in the Midland Counties. Sometimes called with us, though less frequently, *Royston Dick*' [AEB]

sinkfoin, Clare's spelling (and pronunciation?) of sainfoin, a pink-flowered leguminous plant (see *The Poems of John Clare*, ed. J. W. Tibble [London: Dent, 2 vols., 1935], Vol. II, p. 361.)

sprent, sprinkled [AEB]

stock dove, wild pigeon

swaily, shady [GS]

swee, swing [GS]
thrift, '*Armeria maritima* (...Sea-pink, Cliff clover, Ladies' cushions, Heugh daisy) ...The compact pink-flowered cushions grow on sand-dunes, shingle, marshland edges, cliffs, even stone walls near the sea... blooms can vary from deep pink to white, and they have been a favourite for garden edging at least as far back as the sixteenth century' [RM]
throstle, song-thrush [GS]
tim'ly, probably 'timidly' elided, but could also be 'timely' (p. 5)
totter-grass, Quaking-grass [GS], *Briza media* [RM]
Walk'erd, Walkherd Farm, three miles north-east of Tickencote in Rutland, home of Martha ('Patty') Clare (née Martha Turner) before marriage to Clare on 16th March 1820. See Lines, Rodney, 'John Clare's Rutland', *Rutland Record*, 13 (1993), 104–7.
water blabs, marsh marigold (see 'kingcup' above)
Wedgwood, Josiah Wedgwood, English potter, 1730–95
Wellington, Wellington, Arthur Wellesley, 1st Duke of, English statesman and soldier, 1769–1852
whimpling, rippling (see John Clare, *The Rural Muse,* 2nd edition, ed. R.K.R Thornton (Ashington: MidNAG/Carcanet, 1982), p. 158.
yarrow, *Achillea millefolium,* 'flat flower-heads are usually white, but quite often pale (and occasionally dark) pink' [RM]. Confirmation from Clare's 'The Yarrow': 'Some blushing into pink and others white' (p. 78). Long history of use as a herb.
yoe, ewe

INDEX

(Titles in capitals)

A dewdrop on a rose leaf	6
A SPRING MORNING	6
A WALK ('Being refreshed with thoughts of wandering moods')	99
A WALK ('The thorn tree just began to bud')	20
A weedling wild on lonely lea	8
A WILD NOSEGAY	13
A WOODLAND SEAT	70
And though thou seemst a weedling wild	2
ANOTHER SPRING: THE CRAB TREE	67
BALLAD ('A weedling wild on lonely lea')	8
BALLAD ('The spring returns, the pewet screams')	59
Being refreshed with thoughts of wandering moods	99
CHILDHOOD	23
Come Eliza and Anna lay by top and ball	39
Cowslip bud so early peeping	6
Delightful flower 'tis seldom mine	53
Dweller in pastoral spots, life gladly learns	78
Fairy elves, those minute things	19
Field thoughts to me are happiness and joy	94
FIELD THOUGHTS	94
FIRST SIGHT OF SPRING	75
Hail to the violet! Sweet careless spread	5
HEAVY DEW	81
IDLE HOUR	65

In schoolboy days as on a mother's breast	91
Lady 'tis thy desire to move	87
Leaves from eternity are simple things	50
March wakened in wildness	37
May-time is in the meadows coming in	48
Mild health I seek thee, whither art thou found?	21
O native scenes, nought to my heart clings nearer	12
ON SEEING SOME MOSS IN FLOWER EARLY IN SPRING	57
ON SOME FRIENDS LEAVING A FAVOURITE SPOT	15
OPEN WINTER	95
PLEASANT SPOTS	76
Pleasures lie scattered all about our way	77
Poesy now in summer stoops	61
Ragwort thou humble flower with tattered leaves,	79
Sauntering at ease I often love to lean	65
SCRAPS OF SUMMER	68
SONG ('Swamps of wild rush beds and slough's squashy traces')	10
SONNET: FOREST FLOWERS	73
SONNET: TO A RED CLOVER BLOSSOM	7
Spontaneous flourisher in thickets lone	80
SPORT IN THE MEADOWS	48
SPRING ('The sweet spring now is coming')	84
Spring comes anew and brings each little pledge	67
Spring cometh in with all her hues and smells	66
SUMMER BALLAD	61
Swamps of wild rush beds and slough's squashy traces	10
Sweet bottle-shaped flower of lushy red	7
THE ANNIVERSARY, TO A FLOWER OF THE DESERT	37
THE BRAMBLE	80
THE CLUMP OF FERN	77
The common woodbine in the hedgerow showers	82
The daisy is a happy flower	102
The daisy wan, the primrose pale	22
THE DAISY	102

The dreary fen a waste of water goes	98
THE ETERNITY OF NATURE	50
THE EVENING PRIMROSE	72
THE EVERGREEN ROSE	53
THE FEAR OF FLOWERS	74
The hazel blooms in threads of common hue	75
THE HEDGE WOODBINE	82
THE HOLIDAY WALK	39
The humble flower that buds upon the plain	9
The little paths are printed every one	96
The night hath hung the morning smiles in showers	81
The nodding oxeye bends before the wind	74
THE NOSEGAY OF WILD FLOWERS	91
The past it is a magic word	23
THE POESY OF FLOWERS	69
THE PRIMROSE BANK	54
THE PRIMROSE, A SONNET	1
THE RAGWORT	79
The southwest wind how pleasant in the face	68
The spring returns, the pewet screams	59
The sweet spring now is coming	84
The thorn tree just began to bud	20
The water lilies on the meadow stream	83
THE YARROW	78
The yellow lambtoe I have often got	13
There is a wild and beautiful neglect	76
There's the daisy, the woodbine	14
Though thou wert not the place of my being and birth	15
Thrice welcome sweet summer in softness returning	11
'Tis spring day roams with flowers	54
TO A COWSLIP EARLY	6
TO AN INSIGNIFICANT FLOWER OBSCURELY BLOOMING IN A LONELY WILD	2
TO E. L. E. ON MAY MORNING	87
TO THE VIOLET	5
VALENTINE ('A dewdrop on a rose leaf')	86

Violet – thou art a holy blossom	4
Welcome pale primrose starting up between	1
What would the rosey be but as the rose?	69
When milking comes then home the maiden wends	97
When once the sun sinks in the west	72
Where slanting banks are always with the sun	95
Within this pleasant wood beside the lane	70
Wood walks are pleasant every day	57
Ye simple weeds that make the desert gay	73